# Daphne's Dance

# Daphne's Dance

## True Tales in the Evolution of Woman's Sexual Awareness

### AS

14 Boomer Fem Explore Sex From
*Good Girl* Myth to Sexual Revolution,
From Capacity to Fulfillment,
From Patriarchy to Consciousness

## Brigitta Olsen, Ph.D

ISyn Publications
Altadena, California

Copyright © 2009 ISyn Publications

Library of Congress Control Number: 2009911147

Olsen, Brigitta
Daphne's Dance: True tales in the revolution of women's sexual awareness
/ by Brigitta Olsen, PhD

ISBN-13: 978-0-9842117-0-8
ISBN-10: 0-9842117-0-5

Library of Congress data:
Women's sexuality. Sex study women. Evolution of consciousness. Sexual revolution.


Cover art by Corey Petersen.
Original photograph of The Dancing Tree courtesy Carol Lynn Fraser, B.Ed.




This book printed on acid-free paper.

Printed in the United States of America

# Table of Contents

# Preface

I was about five years old when I first wanted to know everything I could about the secret places in my body—the places I wasn't supposed to touch, talk about, show anyone or scratch in public. If I wasn't supposed to know about it, then for sure I wanted to.

I evolved, even matured a little, but my interest in women's sexuality has never waned. After all, I is one! I followed several paths in my personal exploration, including Tantric and Taoist sexual yoga, seeking to understand some 'truth' about woman's sexual capacity.

I became a professional sex and sensuality counselor in 1977 and have worked in this area off and on since. My goal has always been to help people explore the higher reaches of sexual ecstasy.

All women have seen and experienced the effects of double sexual standards for men and women. Like the women in this study, I was raised to be a good girl, came of age in the late sixties, partied hearty in the seventies, then settled into getting on with life—raising kids, supporting them, marriage, divorce, career.

I've resisted playing the role of 'sexpert' with all its social connotations. How people learn, consciousness itself, these questions really intrigue me. Yet every time I consider what it means to be *authentic*, sexuality puts itself high on the list of things to think about.

Woman's sexual capacity is still a taboo subject. Titillation is okay and women's magazines can list the 'Seven most important tricks to satisfy your man.' 'Fix-it' is also okay as long as the focus is on sexual dysfunction.

We still know very little about the high end of the spectrum. We do not have serious social discussion and investigation into the role of woman's profound sexual capacity in the evolution of our species. It is taboo. I guess I'm still that five-year-old at heart because that is where my interests lay.

The idea for this book began years ago on a laughter- and wine-filled evening with two close friends. We started with a group idea for the newest 'bad girl tell-all' bestseller, chronicling a generation's transformation from good girls to titillating bad girls.

When I actually interviewed a few women, they changed my focus. Here was an opportunity to listen to seasoned women tell their sexual stories from the vantage point of 40+ years experience each. While their stories might titillate, they could also shed light on a subject long buried under rules and taboos designed to control and constrain women, often by keeping them from talking to each other.

The deeper I listened, the more I heard a new *woman's wisdom* emerging. Their stories become a glimpse at an evolving definition of good girl, growing out of and beyond outdated Victorian and patriarchal constraints.

Over the years, I have consulted every source I could lay my hands on focused on this subject, too many to name. All of them helped me listen better to what these wise women were saying.

In the first chapter, I depended on Leonard Shlain's **Sex, Time and Power,** to understand woman's sexuality in the context of nature. He clearly places woman's sexuality in the forefront of human evolution and elucidated the many ways women's sexual capacity is unique in all of nature.

For years, his work has led me to speculate on why Nature gave such sexual gifts to women and the profound effect of prolonged ecstatic states on the evolution of consciousness itself. The myth of Daphne kept coming into my thoughts.

According to ancient Greek mythology, Cupid was angry at Apollo for his boastfulness. He shot two poisoned darts, one at Apollo that made him sexually insatiable. The other he shot at Daphne, making her sexually frigid. As Apollo chased her and attempted to rape her, Daphne morphed herself into a laurel tree to escape him. Apollo, in frustration, tore off her branches and created a laurel crown for himself.

Does this myth speak to the beginnings of patriarchy and male dominance over woman's sexuality? Historically, the timing is right. Are we at the other end of that cycle, when Daphne can emerge back into her true, full sexual nature, encouraged by men who are not afraid of her capacity?

Something happened in the 1970s... but was it a real sexual revolution? The Pill certainly changed how many young women approached their own freedom to say yes (or no) to sex, without fear of unwanted pregnancy.

The Pill ripped out political, religious and social controls over women's sexual behavior ... but after the 70s were over, and HIV/AIDS curtailed the excesses of free love, had political, religious and social minds changed? Had *women* changed?

While the Pill and modern medicine had been the instigation for a decade of supposed free love, they also changed the foundation on which we as a species can now deal with woman's sexuality.

> *For the first time in human history, written or otherwise, women are unshackled from the joint fears of unwanted pregnancy and maternal mortality. Now is a significant turning point in the evolution of gender politics and perhaps the evolution of consciousness.*

**Part I She Can** provides perspective on the spectrum of woman's sexual behavior. First, we look at what society told these women they were *supposed to be* sexually—the historical context for defining a *good girl* in the mid-twentieth century. We then balance that view by looking at what a woman's body is *capable of experiencing* sexually—a bigger picture of her *innate sexual capacity*, focusing on what makes human females so different from all other sexually reproducing females in nature.

**Part II She Does** contains the complete transcripts of these fourteen interviews. Mid-career, I completed a Ph.D. in Adult Learning—how the brain works and how best to facilitate learning among adults. It seems that the most complex task of the *human* brain is understanding story.

It makes sense. Our brains evolved and expanded around the campfire, when the ability to conceptualize, through *listening to story*, could easily be the difference between life and death. Therefore, the stories are presented in whole, with minimal editing, so the reader may experience their full gestalt.

All the women interviewed are over fifty, Boomers who started out *good girls* then became sexual rebels, remaining sexually active through menopause and beyond. Most of the women didn't know each other or me before the interview. Granted, fourteen is a very small sample that doesn't necessarily represent all women. However, the threads these women weave are themes familiar to most of us.

With laughter, tears, occasional outrage and wisdom, these crones speak candidly to other crones, to daughters and granddaughters, as well as to lovers and partners. They explore their own bodies, what's endearing and annoying about sex, what works and doesn't work getting to orgasm. Best of all, they shine a bright light into a more authentic future for women.

**Part III She Learns** is first a *quantitative analysis* of what the women said, included at the request of early readers who wanted a horizontal look at the interviews—how many said this or that, did this or that, thought the other. That makes sense too, because woman's sexuality has been taboo for so long, women don't often get to learn from each other.

The final chapter is a *qualitative analysis*, including my own conclusions about the significance of redefining a good girl for today. My thoughts are based on these, my own experience and thirty years counseling/teaching about higher ecstatic states.

This book arises out of its own dance out of the dance of women. Naturally I have honed and shaped, but I have fought hard to preserve the flow, the passion, the wildness, and the sudden naked truths that spring from letting in the light.

May we continue to live in interesting times. Enjoy.

Brigitta Olsen, 2009
Altadena, California

This research is dedicated to my mother, first and foremost a Victorian lady, who evolved herself and shared what she learned with me. Late in life, her mantra became 'Nothing ventured, nothing gained.' She is, in my mind, every woman everywhere—Daphne.

This study is also for all women courageous enough to venture into their own unknown sexual territory that is woman's special capacity, gift and emerging responsibility.

My love and gratitude to all the friends who participated in creating this study—first, the wonderful wise women who bared their sexual secrets to me. And of course without good friends, the project wouldn't have happened. Sheila and Lee, Annie and Peter, Lise, Jules, Irene and Carl supported the project, and me, in all the ways that matter.

Thank you.

# Part I

# She Can

"Now there you have an example of man's reasoning powers, as he calls them. He observes certain facts. For instance, that in all his life he never sees the day that he can satisfy one woman; also, that no woman ever sees the day she can't overwork, and defeat, and put out of commission any ten masculine plants that can be put to bed to her. He puts those strikingly suggestive and luminous facts together and from them draws this astonishing conclusion: The Creator intended the woman to be restricted to one man ... Now if you or any other really intelligent person were arranging the fairnesses and justices between a man and a woman, you would give the man a one fiftieth interest in one woman, and the woman a harem. Now wouldn't you? Necessarily, I give you my word, this creature with the decrepit candle has arranged it exactly the other way. "

Mark Twain

"From women's eyes this doctrine I derive:
They sparkle still the right Promethean fire:
They are the books, the arts, the academes
That show, contain, and nourish all the world."

William Shakespeare Love's Labours Lost

# 1

# Daphne's Choices

*"Homo sapiens means 'Wise Man.' So much greater were the changes in the female of the new species than those of the male that it would have been more accurate for scientists to have named our genus and species Gyna sapiens rather than Homo sapiens.*

**Leonard Shlain, MD, _Sex, Time and Power_**

Does being a *good girl* relate to being authentically sexually fulfilled? There are many stories in myth, fiction and history of women who used seduction and sexuality to influence human affairs. Think of Cleopatra, who used sex to try to save her empire, and Helen of Troy, who threw aside her empire for love—good girls or bad? Was Eve a *good girl* for using her sexuality? Was the Virgin Mary a *good girl* for not using her sexuality? Goddess, priestess, witch or bitch—defining what is *good* for a woman to actually *do sexually* appears to depend on who writes the story.

This chapter focuses on creating context for the concept of *good* female sexual behavior by first looking at a brief historical perspective on *good girl* as evidenced in sexual morés and research, and second, unveiling a woman's innate sexually capacity as it has evolved naturally, speculating that nature's design is probably the healthiest and therefore most innately *good*.

## Historically speaking

For millennia men (and women) have brutally killed other women for sexual behavior. Parents kill their own daughters for the disgrace of getting themselves raped—but don't kill the rapist. Under these circumstances, *good* evolves to mean, 'Be constantly afraid of your own body. Cover it completely.'

*Good* for a priestess during Egyptian, Greek, Roman or pagan times meant using sex to symbolically fertilize the earth's abundance with her own sexual joy in mating. *Good* for some African women meant (and still means) being a eunuch for life so she won't *like* sex and perhaps stray towards another man.

# 4  Daphne's Dance

*Good* for our own Victorian grandmothers and great grandmothers meant *enduring* sex ... but never ever liking it ... or at least never admitting she liked it. One has to wonder about Queen Victoria herself, though, who birthed enough babies to indicate some affinity with the act.

At the beginning of the 20$^{th}$ century, Havelock Ellis attempted to overturn Victorian sexual morés, but actually threatened his own revolution. He claimed that, because women have more sexual organs (vagina, womb, breasts as well as clitoris, compared to the penis), therefore women are more highly sexual beings than men—'their brains are in their wombs!' He tried to transform women into the supreme representation of sexual objects, creatures so pre-occupied with their sexual needs as to be incapable of functioning in any other capacity.

At the same time, he believed that women are innately passive sexually, in order to increase sexual desire in themselves and in males. A woman's modesty and passivity are instinctual and properly defines her place in the larger social order.

Alfred Kinsey, in the 1930s and 40s, wanted to demystify sex, believing it lacked the emotionally demonic potential Freud pushed so hard. In all his reports, based on thousands of interviews, Kinsey never asked why sex was so emotionally loaded, while that is all Freud asked.

Prior to Kinsey, sexual theorists assumed that we are born with a limited amount of orgasms for life and therefore masturbation is a sinful waste. Freud believed that masturbation and anything other than a vaginal orgasm represented psychic immaturity and a 'narcissistic fixation of the libido.'

Kinsey's research supported the opposite—the earlier and more often a woman masturbated, the more orgasms she experienced throughout her life and especially into maturity. Women who did not masturbate and/or indulge in sexual 'petting' before marriage were more likely to be frigid as wives. Highly religious women had less sex and significantly fewer were orgasmic.

Kinsey believed that men had higher sex drives than women. Women in his study reported that talk and pornography during sex were distracting to them, so he also concluded that women are more into the body and physical sensations than men, for whom sex is a greater mind/fantasy trip.

Kinsey's first set of sexual research, about men, was received widely and eagerly in 1948. His second book in 1952, on women, created a huge uproar, much of it because he said women masturbate.

Masters and Johnson followed him in 1960, focusing heavily on the idea that men and women are actually autonomous and self-reliant sexually—meaning that, because of masturbation, which they saw as very good for everyone's general health, women don't really *need* men to be sexually fulfilled, even though they may *want* a man as a partner. And vice versa.

They proposed that women have just as absolute a right to orgasm as men do, and that skillful male lovers by necessity must learn ejaculatory control.

They concluded that men must relinquish their control over sexual response—the traditional assumption that orgasm and sexual pleasure belong solely in the male dominion.

All of these theorists were highly influential in shaping public opinion about who was a *good girl* and who wasn't. Freud and Ellis strongly believed that sex for women belonged in the committed love-bond of marriage—that as long as sex was a mystery, it remained sacred. They felt that demystifying sex trivialized it, profaned it and eliminated the potential for ecstasy itself. Kinsey was at the opposite end of the spectrum from the 'romantics', believing that physical and spiritual passions are not connected. Masters and Johnson positioned themselves somewhere in the middle of those two viewpoints.

This was the stage onto which the Boomer girls were born. Despite the sexual theorists, researchers and philosophers, sex was still a taboo subject for girls. In the years after World War II, *good* must have included a whole lot of sex, given the Boomer generation it spawned, but parents and society trained young girls in the 1950s in a pre-war propriety, as they had been.

A girl learned what was respectable by what she was allowed to wear, what words she could use, what she could read, who she could be with, how she could behave. She wasn't allowed knowledge of her own body, including in most cases anything about menstruation.

She learned the good girl/bad girl myth at home, at school, at church, in the community, on the radio and in the new medium of TV. It became the root metaphor for this generation—grow up to be Beaver Cleaver's mom and you would be *good.* And ... if you're *good* enough, Mr. Right will show up to take care of you. Grow up *bad* and you will come to a very bad end—the femme fatale.

Sometime in the 60s, all that training began to unravel. The Pill had arrived. Women in great numbers wrenched control over their bodies back from others—mainly mothers, fathers, husbands and priests. For the first time in human history, the fear of unwanted pregnancy was reliably gone. Women revealed themselves openly as sexual beings.

This generation redefined *good girl* into a decade of free love, women's liberation and talk of sexual revolution. Boomer women wanted to know more about their bodies, their clitorises, their **capacity** for sexual pleasure. In workshops, they looked at their clitorises and vaginas with hand mirrors. The genie was out of the bottle. Sex *and* sexual pleasure became acceptable *to women themselves.* The Boomer girls still wanted Mr. Right, like their mothers had, but insisted on sampling the goods before they bought.

## 6  Daphne's Dance

**Her Natural Orgasmic State**

Our society continues to apply the medical model to woman's sexuality, focusing on dysfunction, the illusive orgasm, and numbers of contractions.— academic considerations contrasted by a media obsessed with visual titillation.

Even so, we know fairly precisely how much water a body needs daily to stay healthy, as well how much air, nutrients, sleep, exercise. Are these more or less natural than sex? Is there an *innate truth* about what is good or bad sexual behavior for a woman? How many orgasms daily-weekly-monthly are healthy?

It turns out nature has put a huge amount of evolutionary effort into this area, way beyond sex as a tool for procreation. Human females are so radically different, sexually, from all other primate females that monkeys, rats and tigresses don't tell us much about ourselves sexually. Nature clearly focused this energy on human females alone.

Men are a lot like other primate males—they respond to sexual signals with increased testosterone production and readiness to mate. Men do distinguish themselves, however, by having the highest levels of testosterone in nature—pretty much all the time.. Also, there is no correspondence in the wild for male sexual aggression against females, misogyny, self-flagellation or suicide.

The facts listed below come from Leonard Shlain, doctor and author of **Sex, Time and Power.** Dr. Shlain provided clues to the remarkable sexual physiology and capacity nature gave woman. His findings are briefly summarized. If we start to understand her natural capacity, perhaps we can better decide what is or should be *good* behavior for her.

**Her Estrus**

In nature, 269 species of sexually reproducing primate females come into heat, present themselves to an appropriate male, attracting his attention with scent, gesture, call, touch and/or the glorious sight of her engorged genitals. The male's testosterone level rises in response, they mate, and then each goes back to whatever they had been doing. Sometimes, she eats his head. (Actually only insects do that, while for primates, mating is fairly matter of fact.)

For one species, us, it's gotten a bit more complicated. A woman signals sexual readiness **when she chooses, to whom she chooses, at whatever level of intensity she chooses.** She has the ability, different from all her sister species, to say *no* to sex even when she is in heat. Men are sexually ready 24/7. Sometimes this causes problems.

One advantage of this ability is that she has more control over her sexual urges and therefore over when and with whom she conceives . . . and therefore more control over how often she exposes herself to dying in childbirth, a very common occurrence until recently.

Historically one in four women died in childbirth until the mid-1900s. Saying no to sex meant she had more probability of living to raise her existing children to self-reliance.

*At the same time she can say no at will, she also can say yes at will! Woman has the capacity to consciously turn on her sexual switch. No other females on earth can do that.*

When living in family groups and villages, women often cycle their periods and therefore estrus, at the same time. This ability has important implications in gender politics.

In nature, when the male is disproportionately larger than the female, he fights for mating privileges with other males, while keeping 'his' females under control. Female estrus cycles tend to be staggered over time, providing constant sex for the alpha male.

We see more sexual cooperation and monogamy when males and females are closer in size and weight. Then, females cycle in unison and they break the back of a reproductive system that rewards the fiercest, strongest males with a sexual monopoly over the gene pool—as one male cannot possibly satisfy all the females at once. When females living closely together synchronize their menses, they also enhance social equality with males.

Where females in nature have 24/7 sexual receptivity, no species exhibits monogamous behavior.

However, for us, this sexual capacity has raised male jealousy to a 'staggering waste of spirit,' requiring huge amounts of legal, religious and cultural barriers to regulate male sexual competition. This becomes blaming her for being herself, perhaps another clue to the *good girl/ bad girl* myth.

### Facts:

A human female is unique in nature in that she can choose not to have sex when she is in heat.

She can and does hide the fact that she is in heat from males and often from herself.

### Facts:

When groups of females synchronize their estrus, they enhance social standing while adding diversity to the gene pool.

No females who are ready for sex 24/7 are naturally monogamous.

## Just the Facts, Ma'am

There are some 300,000 sexually reproducing species on the earth. Of those, 6,000 are mammals. Of those, some 269 are primates like us.

The human female differs from *all others* in that she:

- has cryptic/hidden ovulatory signals, including no coarse odor or sounds, body stance, facial expressions or gesticulations, or visible color change

- experiences continual 24/7 sexual receptivity

- has the *capacity* to say no to sex during ovulation—when she is in heat

- has a functioning clitoris, the only organ in nature designed purely for pleasure

- can cycle her estrus in harmony with other women

- has an exceedingly high death rate from child birth

- experiences healthy and often enhanced sexual functioning after menopause

- if healthy, can live a third or more of her life after menopause—that is, she becomes a grandmother . . . while remaining sexually active

## Her Clitoris

The clitoris is high on the list of unique organs in nature. It is the only organ whose sole purpose seems to be pleasure. Although the female bonobo chimp has a rudimentary clitoris, she doesn't appear to get the same levels of pleasure that the human female can … and often does.

The tip of the clitoris is the most concentrated collection of nerve endings in anybody's body, anywhere on earth, including the penis, with over 8,000 sensitive dendrites. The penis has the same number of nerves but spread over a larger area.

To what end, all these densely packed nerve endings? The benefits of male pleasure are obvious—he arouses, mates and delivers his seed to continue the species. Nature rewards him with seven to nine seconds of intense pleasure—the male orgasm. He is driven to repeat this behavior as often as he can find a willing female.

According to Shlain's speculations, nature evolved the clitoris to entice women to have sex. That may sound funny, as females in nature don't seem to need a lot of enticing once estrus starts. It's a different story for woman.

*Facts:*

External female genitalia are rare in nature.

An organ devoted solely to pleasure is unique in nature.

8000 nerve endings concentrated in a 1-2 square inch area is unique in nature.

She has known the connection between sex and babies for a long time, possibly 40,000 to 60,000 years. She figured out that if she had sex, she could easily die in childbirth, for maternal mortality rates in humans are the highest of any in nature—we're still evolving into the upright posture of bipedalism, with narrow hips and the bigger brain size of our species.

For every male who died battling the saber tooth tiger so he could bring home the bacon, there was a woman who died in childbirth. Just imagine the genetic memory. For tens of thousands of years, *every time* she contemplated sex, she had to weigh her desire for pleasure against her probable death and that of her existing dependent children.

*Good girl* takes on two conflicting meanings then, in nature—the one who stays alive or the one who perpetuates the species. Nature needed to sweeten the pleasure pot *a lot* in order to overcome a woman's good common sense and survival instincts.

And sweeten the pot Mother Nature did! Women are capable of hours-long continuous orgasmic states, **after** being warmed up by multiple orgasms.

## Her Non-orgasm

**Facts:**

Female animals rarely die in childbirth. One in four human females died in childbirth, until the last 60 years.

A human female can enjoy sex when she is already pregnant or breast-feeding or post-menopausal.

It is a tricky business to shed light on the real or imagined limits to a woman's sexual capacity. Mainstream science and medicine focus on 'that pesky orgasm'— their need to fix a perceived dysfunction. Often they describe what is normal for a woman in terms of what is normal for a man. Most women haven't a clue what their full capacity for sexual expression is.

It is possible the metaphorical chickens are coming home to roost. Some researchers claim that 50% of today's women don't orgasm at all. Whoa! Does that seem natural, given all the equipment nature evolved just for her to enjoy?

A woman's heat—sexual desire—is a subtle field of hormonal energy and easily knocked out of balance. It could be our environment is so toxic (air and water pollution, electromagnetic fields crossing everywhere, chemically-laden foods) that her body's chemistry is seriously disturbed.

It could be the *good girl* brainwashing has been too effective and *good girls* don't have sex at all. But, you say, Madison Avenue marketers use a woman's body to sell everything from cars to Burger King Whoppers, so *good girl* messages have surely been overwhelmed as the media somewhat trivially defines what a 'right' woman should look like and do.

It could be that 50% of recent generations of women still believe what their mothers told them as children—'Don't touch yourself there, it's nasty!' What happens when girls don't touch themselves as children and adolescents? They don't experience many orgasms throughout life. Is nature's gift of being uniquely orgasmic a 'use it or lose it' proposition for women, that must be triggered early in life?

It could be these media messages are so pervasive and contradictory, that she isn't interested in knowing any more—the rewards aren't worth the effort and it is so easy to fake an orgasm and still catch your man.

At the same time, pornography is the most popular and profitable industry in all forms of media, including the internet. Well over 10 million women are bound up in sexual slavery in the United States alone.

The model for women to judge their bodies by is a neutered, anorexic 'boy with breasts.' Therefore, a woman or young girl sees few messages encouraging her to explore her sexuality in healthy ways.

Losing orgasmic functioning could be a result of the women's liberation movement. Women moved into the workplace in droves during the 1980s. In the process, fashions included junior men costumes—suits and ties. As women competed to be like men in the workplace arena, they often brought it home to the bedroom where competition is not very satisfying.

In the 1950s, according to Kinsey, women orgasmed twice as long as men, on average. Yet today, fifty years later, 50% of women don't orgasm at all. Many of my female clients who do orgasm described their experience as being 'just like a man'. It could be that she doesn't know her capacity is greater than that.

Today we take for granted that a woman will raise children *and* have a career. Stress levels are at an all time high in hectic multi-tasking households. She works full time, raises the kids, plays soccer mom, shops, cleans, cooks and pays the bills. Who has time or energy to relax, feel her body, and explore her sensuality in preparation for a night of fully-aroused love-making?

For all these reasons, 50% of women may be non-orgasmic—and that could be depressing for the rest of us. The eras in recorded history when the power elite has loosened the shackles on women's sexuality, just a bit, have also been epochs of major advances in civilization—in art, letters, science and philosophy. Greek, Roman and Egyptian cultures come to mind, as well as the Italian Renaissance.

**Possible reasons for dysfunction:**

Environmental toxins

Brainwashing

Trivialized media messages about sex

Lack of knowledge

Highly stressful lifestyle

So what does the positive, pleasurable side of this coin look like, for the 50%, or more, of women who are orgasmic?

## Prolonged Ecstatic States

*The piece de resistance in our small corner of the universe is the human female orgasm. There is nothing else like it in nature.*

Throughout history, men have written about the phenomenon of the fully aroused women as being either *very sacred or very scary*. One can picture Cleopatra, Nefertiti, Eleanor of Aquitaine, Helen of Troy—women of privilege and power, allowed by their station in the world to fully arouse their passions in order to control powerful men.

Most women have the capacity to experience these profound, prolonged orgasmic states if they are not physically impaired. It can last for hours and sometimes days. Libido may determine if she *chooses* to pursue this experience (different from her physical capacity to experience). Libido here means *desire* for sexual fulfillment, determined by body chemistry.

When a woman is in a prolonged ecstatic state, her brain shuts off the fear centers, indicating her willingness to trust. Her body floods with hormones and healing/happy chemicals that slow the aging process, while flooding her brain with a sense of well-being that can last long after the sex act itself.

The most important of these hormones is oxytocin, a master hormone regulator affectionately nicknamed the 'cuddle hormone' in today's media. Oxytocin supports pair bonding in her brain—with a child during breast feeding and with a lover during sex. A woman literally connects energetically, chemically and emotionally to whoever stimulates her body to release oxytocin.

Once she feels trust and experiences sufficiently skilled foreplay to open this particular spigot, she *bonds* to that person, emotionally and chemically. Women can participate in prolonged ecstatic states even when they are not ovulating (in heat) so the bonding is not necessary *just* for providing a father for her children.

At the same time, her body's receptivity to sperm and therefore conception is intimately dependent on how turned on and fulfilled she is by the experience. So pleasure is necessary for perpetuating the species but perpetuating the species is not necessary for pleasure.

Clearly nature did not evolve human female sexuality strictly for reproduction. Add to it that women with multiple births tend to have multiple orgasms more often than women with one or no births. What is nature thinking?

Throughout the ages, some sexual philosophers, usually in non-patriarchal cultures, have taken the sacred route to understanding woman's sexual capacity, concluding that a woman's body is itself the bridge to the divine. In pre-Confucian Taoist China for example, the spiritual leaders were women, known as the Immortal Sisters. An Immortal Sister learned to turn her body into a conduit for Divine Energy, refining her ability to transmute that intense sexual energy into healing, spiritual advancement and wisdom. Hindu and Buddhist Tantric studies are similarly energy-based.

A trained priestess in many societies is expected to connect directly with the primal energy of the universe, interceding on behalf of her people. Oftentimes, at the peak of her sexual ecstasy, she mates with a man, who can then experience this same ecstatic state. Together, they symbolically fertilize the earth itself.

Most major religions reached similar conclusions about women's sexuality over the last 5,000 years, although most carefully couched that knowledge as 'mystery traditions,' available to the power elite only. (Maybe it isn't an accident that many women cry, 'Oh God, oh God' when in the throes of passion?)

Could it be that when we look beyond local gender politics, the *good girl* is the one who studies her sexuality, constantly striving for higher and higher ecstatic and therefore sacred states?

Where is the bar, when it comes to orgasms? Is it normal, and therefore *good*, for a woman to orgasm, or not to orgasm? How many times? For how long? We don't know.

## Her Grandmother

In nature, a female has her last estrus, mates and bears her last offspring. She lives only long enough to raise it/them to independence, and then she dies. She does not mate anymore and she does not live beyond the time when she needs to be a viable mother.

*Characteristics of post-menopausal woman:*

Sudden rise in testosterone

Clear-headed assertiveness

Focus on life goals, resolve

Better spatial awareness and sense of direction

More force of character, aggression and dominance

We, on the other hand, have grandmothers. Women live on average one-half to three-fifths of their lives before and *after* they are sexually reproducing. To top it off, a post-menopausal woman tends to experience bigger and better orgasms as she matures, and because bigger and better orgasms promote health and slow the aging process, she could live a very vibrant and long old age if she stays sexually active.

She may have fewer partners to choose from, though. Many witty pundits have remarked on this irony—men peak sexually at 15, women peak at 39. By 50, many men lose a significant amount of their staying power in sex, gradually losing the ability to achieve an erection. It does seem like poor planning or maybe a bad joke on someone's part . . . unless the goal of all that sexual energy in a mature woman is for a purpose we haven't uncovered yet.

It could also be that it takes that long for men to lose some of their *urgency to ejaculate*. By 40, he might be willing to slow down enough to put authentic sexual attention on her. For the over-50 crowd, his sexuality may have slowed way down, while her orgasms are getting bigger and better. Is nature making it easier for him to participate in her ecstatic energy?

Are we any closer to understanding what a *good girl* is after this brief foray into a woman's physical capacity for sexual expression as well as her profound differences with all other females in nature? Let's summarize:

- a woman has a hidden estrus, from herself and males, and has the ability to say no to sex when she is in heat, allowing her to choose when and with whom she has sex
- a woman has a developed clitoris, a unique organ designed only for pleasure
- a woman has the capacity for orgasm, multiple orgasms and prolonged hours-long ecstatic orgasms, consistently longer and more intense than a male's
- a woman can consciously decide to turn on her sexual switch
- a woman has a far higher probability of dying in childbirth than any other female in nature—one in four—without intervention
- a woman can live to be a grandmother and experience enhanced orgasmic states after she is incapable of bearing children

It would seem we traded 'natural' reproductive sex for the capacity for prolonged ecstatic states. Nature clearly designed her body for pleasure, as well as for reproduction. But, does any of this enlighten us about what a *good girl should do*? Much of that answer lies in the current atmosphere of patriarchy and misogyny.

Shlain sums up the origins of gender politics this way: when woman stood upright, she experienced an increased blood loss, which let to an iron deficiency. She needed a male to slay fresh meat for her and her children, rewarding him with sex outside of estrus. This became an ancient agreement between men and women—men will go first in danger, by protecting and providing with their superior strength, while women will go first in pleasure, with their superior sexual capacity. Both risked their lives in the process.

Any species splits into two genders to increase diversity and to maximize its ability to survive. Both genders must be equal, dependent on each other . . . and different, for the system to work. And men don't seem to like it.

The interesting anomaly for men in this process is that men had to be not only vicious killers, slaying the beasts, but if they wanted sex, they had to be gentle lovers too. Rape has never been a sustainable practice and doesn't really exist in nature.

## Daphne

Remember the Greek myth from the **Preface**, where Cupid darted Apollo so he was sexually insatiable and Daphne so she was frigid? She turned herself into a tree to avoid being raped by Apollo. This myth arose about the time cultures around the world turned to patriarchal systems and men tried to take control over women's sexuality.

Could the sexual revolution of the 1970s be another step in Daphne's Dance, her desire to return from a wooden state to full sensual awareness? Can she take back control over her own sexual expression now, finally freed from male sexual aggression, unwanted pregnancies and the high risk of death by childbirth? If so, then truly we don't know what *good* is ... women have never been free this way within our human memory.

With this brief foray into evolution and history, next listen carefully to real stories from real women who were the first to live through this phase of an extraordinary transformation. Some signposts they give us may be subtle and dim, as we don't know yet what is going to be most important. Others may fairly scream at us.

Each story mirrors the others but dances in its own way. Like Rumi says, 'Read slowly, dance wildly.'

# Part II

# She Does

*"The conceptual boundary between male and female,*
*self and other, dissolves, and—as every spoke leads to the hub—*
*this particular embrace on this particular day discloses itself*
*as going on forever behind the scenes."*

**Alan Watts**

In the following pages we explore the sexual journeys of fourteen Boomer women—from good girl/bad girl myths, to orgasms, to profound ecstatic states—by way of lovers, gender politics, abuse and passion. Like delving through someone's hidden lingerie drawer, they shatter myths about women's innate sexual capacity and how good girls *and* bad girls became good and *wise* women.

All fourteen women are over fifty, all grew up in a 'leave it to beaver' world, all came of age sexually with the Pill, many blazed trails into the predominantly male world of work outside the home and away from traditional homemaker stereotypes.

The most complex task the human brain accomplishes is understanding story, according to Stanford neurophysiologists and computer scientists. Story, with all its layered nuance, core beliefs and root metaphors, has stymied artificial intelligence researchers and pioneers for decades, for this reason.

Listen to these stories as if you are sitting around the village fire at night, wise crones telling their teaching tales. Perhaps the threads they weave can lead future generations of women to understand what an authentically *good girl* is.

# 2

# Katarina

I was a country girl up until eighth grade. We didn't have a bad girl paradigm there because everyone knew everything about everybody. There were more churches per capita than any place else I've ever been. And each one felt they had the right to tell all the others what was wrong with their interpretation of things.

I moved to a city for high school and then definitely encountered the good girl/bad girl paradigm. You were a bad girl if you had breasts and people could see it—you had to dress like your grandmother. If anything showed off your body, you were a slut. And, God forbid, you actually made out with boys. That was really tawdry. I was there for one year and then moved away to a larger city to live with my sister and do childcare for her.

At the metropolitan high school, more of the kids had parents who were educated. There was a much broader spectrum of race, religion, cultural types. We had a Basque community. I met Jews for the first time in my life. We'd had African Americans in my elementary school but they were sharecroppers at the absolute bottom rung of the social order. In high school it was different. I stayed at that school for three years until I graduated—right in time for the Summer of Love!

People definitely talked about good girls and bad girls in high school. When I was the new kid, just coming into the school, I didn't know it was acceptable to 'go together' with a boy. That was real different from what my mother had told me. She'd said that as soon as you get involved with a boy, you lose your motivation to get up and get moving.

The summer between my junior and senior years I became sexually active. I was on the Pill and I thought sex was a great thing. I was sixteen.

\*\*\*

There were several first encounters actually. I was extremely muscular and very very thin and it was impossible for the gentleman to penetrate me. So there were three attempts from three different guys and I quickly became Miss Popularity because I was putting out. That had been a rarity for me.

I enjoyed the sex so much that I kept putting out. Thus I became one of the bad girls and you know, I wasn't concerned with that at all. I found a new set of girlfriends where sex and psychedelics were a way of life. It was a whole new paradigm for me and I had fun with it.

By the time I was out of high school, I was living with a college professor. He and his wife were swingers and talked about sex all the time. And of course they wanted to have sex with me, but they were way too old as far as I was concerned.

I was very fortunate in not contracting any STDs [sexually transmitted diseases] because we used no protection. I was on the Pill, which I was taking to regulate my periods. At the time, I knew I wasn't going to get pregnant but I didn't realize until I actually got pregnant how much fear of pregnancy had been a part of my entire life. I had no idea, no idea … how unconscious the fear of pregnancy was for me.

\*\*\*

My parents never talked about sex. We had farm animals so we witnessed sex all the time. We knew it as a mechanical thing, not as a pair bonding thing. It wasn't until many many years later that my younger sister asked my mother if she had ever had an orgasm. My mother, who was a medical professional, said 'I think I almost did once, but I'm not sure … '

I, on the other hand … have always been orgasmic! My mom always said 'I don't know where you girls get your interest in sex. Your father certainly wasn't interested in sex.' Which of course just made us laugh because then we knew where it came from … but she didn't. Sex was never spoken of as anything desirable. It was bad news.

\*\*\*

At 18, I saw myself as adventuresome sexually. I saw myself like the US politically, which has manifest destiny. 'Hey, we have the Pill. We are supposed to use this and find out what it's all about. It's an advantage we have. Just like getting the vote, we now get the Pill.'

Equal rights amendments and Ms. Magazine and Gloria Steinem and a new sense of women as a powerful force in the world—it all started for me during the Summer of Love.

I saw myself in that whole movement as a player—not a very powerful person but I certainly felt like a New Age explorer. And I certainly wasn't bound by old mores about sexual behavior. Go out to lunch with someone, then go to bed with him. Then go out with someone else in the evening. It was all okay.

However, many of my friends at that time—the more traditional ones that hadn't moved into the hippie scene—were utterly appalled by what I was doing. 'You'll have to pay for this some way'—that was the message they sent me. 'Find a man who'll want to marry you.' The proposals actually came in daily. The message was that then all you had to do was have sex with him.

I lived with someone for five years during college and after. I was monogamous. There came a point when I discovered I preferred, more than anything else, to have consistent good sex with one partner. I split up with him over economic issues and dated many many different guys after that.

I found my most favorite pickup line in the world at that time. When I pulled up to a stoplight next to an appealing guy in a nice car, I'd say 'Hey, do you fool around?' It always worked!

***

I went through a number of fine gentlemen very quickly, really great men that I enjoyed enormously … but I still hadn't found the right guy. And then I met the man who is still my husband—we've been married for 30 years even though we haven't been 'together' for 10 years.

When we separated I just really thought that my sex life was over—that I was an old woman—while he of course was chasing teenagers, one in particular that is younger than our children.

I just… well, after awhile I just figured all guys are like that so I put it to rest in my head and focused my whole attention on my career. Then a couple of years ago I met Mac and had an outstanding sexual relationship with him. He did not want a committed relationship, No, that's not true. He knew he was dying but he didn't say that to me … he didn't tell me at all. He said 'I don't have the luxury of spending time with you. It wears me out and I have to earn a living and I'm wasting time thinking about you.'

It just hurt me deeply … but we continued to play that game as long as we pretended that I was the one attracted to him. Three weeks before he died, we were together and we had great sex. He asked, 'How are you?' I said, 'Physically I'm fine but emotionally I know you're about to put me out the door and I just don't like it.' He said, 'What is it with you? We've been going together for a year and a half. What more do you want?'

And I looked over my shoulder to see if someone else was in the room. I couldn't imagine that what we were doing was going together. When he died I got the most incredible acknowledgement from his friends but I didn't ever get that from him.

It was a total surprise to me that he was going to die. He knew but he never shared it with me. In retrospect it was so obvious. It was only four months ago, so I'm still grieving. I'm starting to get randy again also. He was such an extraordinary lover that I really don't want to dither around. I don't know whether I will be sexually active again or not. Whoever he is will have to be extraordinary too.

The thing about being post-menopausal is that I can take care of any needs I might have … physical needs, that is. Emotional needs—that's different. I've considered getting one of those pillows that's a man's shirt made into a pillow, so his arm can come around me.

*****

What made Mac such an extraordinary lover was that I'd never had a man dedicated to my satisfaction before. And I literally could not walk after sex with him, not from soreness, but from the amount of oxytocin in my blood stream. I would stagger and fall like I was drunk. That's a wonderful place to be! And he was a wonderful man who thought it was his responsibility to take me there. You got hard shoes to fill, Mr. Angel!

My marriage was quite different. We had what I thought was great sex for many years but now I see Fred as one of those dogs that humps everyone's legs. It was indiscriminate—he was indiscriminate. He didn't really care if I was there or not… and I was entirely responsible for taking care of myself. It was not a nurturing relationship. It reminds me of Lenny Bruce's saying 'Men will fuck mud.' Hmmm. In my marriage, I was the mud.

I could have been a knothole in a tree as far as he was concerned. It played out in many different ways—in not looking at me, for instance. He had a huge thing about me having my ears pierced more than once—'No don't do that, it looks cheap. I don't like it.' And so I did it and he didn't even notice for six months.

The sex was fantastic, as long as I took care of myself and as long as I was available for him to use whenever he wanted. It all came to a head when I had a very serious urinary tract infection. It was essential I not have sex as it could turn the infection around and kill me. Fred's concern was 'Well, what about me and my needs?' I realized I was a sperm receptacle. His commitment was to getting off, not to me and not to the relationship.

It became something I wasn't willing to live with anymore. We lived together for two more years, while he did AA and I did Alanon. We did couples counseling together too.

But that was the event that turned the tide for me. He felt that jacking off was not something a married man should have to do—that was my responsibility. And it didn't go both ways—I was still totally responsible for meeting my own sexual needs.

I just went dormant after that. I moved out of our bed and literary just shut myself down for years. I was blown away by what I saw as a complete and utter failure on my part to pick an appropriate partner.

***

I orgasm easily and plentifully. I think having a vibrator as a young woman helped enormously—like having a baseline, a medical baseline. I never even considered, until I was with Mac, that I could come until I was insensible. I mean, orgasming three times had been good and normal for me.

Coming extensively was something new and exciting and wonderful and totally unexpected—especially for someone like me who was used to coming. I just had never even thought there was more to be had—to keep on coming for hours until it's impossible to differentiate any more between one peak and the next. It became an endless wave of pleasure for me with Mac.

He got me there by continuously asking me what I liked. He showed me a totally new way of using my body ... he played my body like a fine instrument, like a cello. And he created scenarios. Like instead of going to bed to have sex, we'd do it on the couch, on the computer table, on the stairs, on a ladder. And he was always asking me, 'Is this okay for you? Is this all right? Do you like it when I do this?'

Literally I think he was the first guy, ever in my life, who was like that. He forced me to tell him what I liked ... every step of the way! You have to be conscious and present here, so that it just gets better, every second, every stroke. He was having some sexual dysfunction towards the end because of the blood pressure issue but it made no difference in our relationship because he was so skillful as a lover, so patient.

It was the first time I ever had a man pull out a vibrator and say, 'Here, use this the way you think is best.' And he was delighted with it, he was thrilled with me pleasing myself. It was satisfying for both of us. He loved it when I would come up with something like, 'There is this magic spot on my neck and you have to kiss it.' 'Where is it?' 'Well, you have to find it.' 'Here?' 'Nope.' 'Here?' 'Nope.' 'Here?' 'Nope.' 'Well, maybe it's not on my neck, maybe it's on my shoulder...'

So there was playfulness. It was never an uncomfortable dialogue. Never. It was the most empowered and empowering dialogue I've ever had in my life.

What a gift he gave me. So few women have a chance at that. At his funeral, there were women and women and women. One of them—I knew who she was from her picture in his bedroom. I could look at his pictures and know which women were his lovers because of their eyes—they have the look, what I call the hungry tiger look.

The last time we were together, he said 'I always get energized after sex with you and I'm not doing that this time. I'm feeling old and tired and I resent the hell out of it.' I said, 'I'm doing fine, there is nothing I need.' But I knew I had to leave and later I knew why. I was literally fucking his brains out.

He was not a playboy. He was honorable. He did not lie. He did not cheat on them or me. Probably thirty women showed up at his memorial service ... his old girlfriends. He didn't stay with them long.

***

I do have fantasies. My favorite is island life ... in the sense that I like being outdoors, making love outdoors. I like feeling the air on my skin. The fantasy is more a visual of an environment than anything else. It doesn't matter who the man is in the fantasy, or the seduction—none of those things matter to me. Give me a massage and oral sex and I'm over the top—you can have anything you want from me.

There is one time that stands out for me, though. My husband and I were trying to get pregnant. It was one of the most fun things I've ever done in my life. I literally got pregnant when I tried to get pregnant but we kept trying for two weeks. That's a paradigm shift right there! When I look at people who try for two years, I'm sure that's terrible ... but for us, those two weeks were absolutely great.

What I like the most about sex is oxytocin. It feels ... like satisfied, the same satisfaction as breast feeding. I have no illusions about sexual satisfaction being a chemical thing—it is a chemical thing! Among the lesbian community there's a joke—'What do lesbians do on a second date? Rent a U-haul and move in!' That's how satisfied lots of oxytocin makes you feel and you never want to leave it.

What I don't like about sex is sleeping on the wet spot. Actually I think seminal fluid is poorly designed. That's the only thing I'd do away with. It's not my flavor or texture, I don't care for it. It's the only annoyance I can think of.

***

There is something I really enjoyed as a young woman that I don't have now—a lack of significance. I have significance now around sex .... I guess I could look at rewriting that story—I would make sex insignificant now, in order to get some more of it. But probably it's the significance that makes it what it is—certainly that was a constant conversation with Mac.

I'm really not looking for a fuck buddy now. I've had that all my life and that's not what I want anymore. So there is a significance that was not there when I was a young woman. Maybe I just don't have enough time anymore.

Mac really changed me and how I think about my sex life. Before I go there again, there's got to be significant trust. The profound state of pleasure he took me to makes the act itself significant, partly because it makes one so very vulnerable. And it wasn't even what I was looking for when I met him. I didn't know it was even possible before Mac, so I could look for it.

The most endearing sex habit to me is calling me the next day to see how I'm doing. 'You okay? How ya doing?'

The least endearing is answering a phone while we're making love. That'll turn me off completely.

There are a few things I won't do. I'm not into multiples. Exhibitionism doesn't hold anything for me. I'm really not interested in porn. At one point I realized, 'Oh my goodness, that might be good for him but I have no interest whatsoever in watching it. Could you turn off the tv please?' I could care less about pornography.

I don't do s&m. I think that's from boys boarding schools where seminal fluid is all they have to work with.

***

There are some differences for me between pre- and post-menopause. There is far less urgency. I have no urgency around sex at all anymore, as a matter of fact. I would say I'm probably slower to arouse, but not significantly.

The good girl/bad girl paradigm itself has changed. I work with kids all the time. I think the paradigm has shifted because of sexually transmitted diseases. Kids don't date one on one anymore, they date in groups, so they are starting to have sex much later than we did. We used to date one guy and one girl and now a group goes on dates.

Today I would define a good girl as someone who is being sexually responsible, using prophylactics and requiring her partner to, as well. She protects herself but she also sets the boundaries for the man.

A good girl gets her education—whether she has sex or not. I remember when girls were told 'An education is a waste on you because you're going to get married and have kids.' That's been blown totally out of the water, and our young women are now told that they can and will do anything that they choose to do.

A girl is good sexually when she enjoys it, when she is authentic. Sex is not to keep someone or to get something from someone. That's kind of an idealistic definition, but it's one I would aspire to have young women understand.

The sexual bad girl? The one who's not being responsible, who's transmitting STDs. I think those people are the most irresponsible people on the planet. I also really dislike the idea of sex as a barter system. I understand that for some people it's all they have to barter with—women and men. But I do not like the idea of sex as barter. I'm sure that's partly my own issues with my husband and his behavior—buying young women. I just think it's so creepy. Many of those young women have no choice. Just because the high end call girls get all the publicity, we think all girls have a choice ... but the high end call girls are the only ones who can say no to anyone they want to.

Now that I'm one of the 'wise women' I get to say that sex is a gift, a divine gift. And I want to say to all the young women—explore it and find what works for you ... what satisfies you ... what defines you. Be open, don't accept someone else's definition of what's good and bad for you—find your own.

# 3

# Lily

I was in high school when I first started having sex. There were some girls that had sex that we all knew were bad girls. And there were other girls having sex that were good girls. So ... what was that all about? Ha-ha!

A good girl would have sex if she was in love. A bad girl would have sex just to have sex. She didn't have to be in love. And she liked a lot of sex ... so she had a lot of it.

Was I one of the bad girls? No, I was one of the good girls ... who concentrated on knowing the bad boys!

It's all so puritanical. It's also very Christian ... The body is to be punished because it's born evil. The body has to be mistrusted. The devil comes to idle hands. But I think it's not only Christian, it's any kind of fundamentalism because it's a very narrow view.

And yet, how intelligent the body is! We're not taught how intelligent the body is. Sexual mores are a way of controlling. We do know why women have been controlled ... and why the powers that be want to control everything. They define what's good, what's bad.

It's like [Marshall] McLuhan says—society's looking at the future through the rear view mirror. But that's what makes a society stable—the bell curve. You can only have so many on the vanguard, a huge middle to support everything and the weirdoes on the other end.

I think it's kind of fun, the whole concept of good girl and bad girl. It's not fun to be good all the time. You have to explore your nature, and it is part of your nature, being bad. I think I've been mostly good, though. Clumsy, but earnest. I can only tell you my story.

***

After I had my high school love affair, I ended up moving in with this guy, which was very rare in those days ... nobody did it ... because I had no family. Then, I followed my father to South East Asia and I lived in Bangkok with an American family, my little sister and I.

And I had the most extraordinary string of affairs with the most remarkable men—that was my real introduction to sex and it was totally brilliant. I learned about the neediness, terrible neediness, of men. How vulnerable, how struck down they were, how they struggled.

I met some strong characters, too. The second man I made love to was a Scottish missionary and it was on the beach in a hut on the Gulf of Siam. We broke up when he wanted to save my soul, on Sunday. And this was at a Presbyterian Church camp.

We used to meet. I would stand on the toilet and look through the chinks in the wall waiting for him to appear. Then we would walk to this little hut made out of palm fronds and bamboo. It was very funny.

My next lover was a German merchant marine, who was very guilty towards Americans about WWII. Terrible guilt. I met him at a party and toured through his ship and then we made love. He was the first one who introduced me to what he called French love, which means he gave me head. And I felt so terribly sorry for him, he had such a sad story.

Even so, I can't say that the earth shook. It wasn't even about that ... and yet it was about that in a way. Was it about love and desire? I didn't love him. I didn't even know if I desired him. I was curious. I was exploring. I was having an adventure.

I think with age everything changes. I fucked a lot of men. And when I look back on it now, I wonder why. What a waste of time. And now what I'm looking for is entirely different, because that for me is no longer an adventure, I know all that already.

Now, I'm looking for the spiritual adventure. If I can get it in a relationship with somebody that includes physical love—great—but I'm not going to wait for that. It's what's necessary for me now. I'm at a different stage in my life.

On one level, I don't give a damn about sex. I love flirtation and I love being desired by men and dancing with them and the whole interchange, but I don't have to be having sex every day. If I felt terribly in love with somebody, I would certainly want to be having sex with them all the time.

But I think that's harder and harder to do as you get older because you know a lot more. You're not as easily fooled and you know the price of almost everything. And what price do you want to pay? Is it worth it? How good is it? And what goes with it?

\*\*\*

Even in marriage. The first time I married was when I came back from Bangkok, so I married the high school sweetheart and I was totally miserable, just like the first time I lived with him. I don't know what I had to find out! We separated because I thought he had been unfaithful to me with college students.

I was working in a government agency, sending him to school on my miserable little Clerk 3 salary. When we separated it was like the sky fell, the whole world fell on my head and all my illusions shattered. I was in great pain for about a year. I married nine days before I was 21 and by 23, we were divorced.

Then I met my second husband and we went to England. It was during the Viet Nam war, when he was escaping the draft. We did a lot of dope and acid and met some fascinating people in London. He screwed a couple of the women. I found out about one of them somehow and it came to pass that I reacted.

So much for two marriages. I had been faithful up to this point while I was married. Then I went to stay with these German women I knew—Astrid and another German girl—it was a very cosmopolitan crowd. We were in this stuffy little flat in Knightsbridge and everybody was putting perfume on all the time and it was very stuffy because the heater was on and it was cold outside and people were on the phone.

One night, those women, at least one of which had screwed my husband, took me out where I met somebody else who was also an artist like my husband (I'm a fall guy for that) and I spent the night with him.

They had set me up! That was my first experience with not being mono-gamous One of them screwed my husband and then they set me up. She said 'Okay, now it's your turn, Honey. Here you go.' And I was going to go back and spend another night with him even though it wasn't terribly interesting sexually but was *very* interesting in other ways.

But one of women called my husband and told him and he came and collected me right away! How strange is all that?

\*\*\*

Ultimately, I believe that if you feel like being with somebody, then be with them. And if you don't, then don't—right?—even if it isn't the best sexually, as long as it's interesting in other ways.

The 'knock 'em dead, jungle bunny, I don't care who you are, just don't stop' kind of sex? It always had a terrible price for me.

On the other hand, let's face it, good sex is like nothing else in the world, it's a fabulous thing. We're engineered for that. It's nature's way, to procreate the species.

Even though we're past menopause, we're still the only species where the females *can* enjoy sex past menopause. We still have a clitoris and we're the only animal with a clitoris! There must be a reason for it and I think it's for bonding.

That's why after you've bonded, for Christ sake, you don't have to keep doing it. You've joined. You have the husband. It doesn't have to be the total stage of your life, not all of your life. You move on.

Margaret Mead said every woman should have three marriages—the first when you are young and know nothing and it's like your first drag of marijuana. And the second marriage is for children. And the third marriage is to enjoy in your old age. Does that make sense, or what?

We all dream of that extraordinary match, that perfect sex, witty conversation and wonderful character. Everything rolled into one, everything our culture talks about as being desirable in sex—good girl/bad girl, good boy/bad boy, gentle but forceful. We're brainwashed into thinking that's what we have to have.

It would take about a hundred men for me to have all that much, which is why I've screwed about a hundred men. Come on! You are never going to have all that in one person, unless you're incredibly lucky and even then there's bound to be something to set you off about him.

It's a total fantasy. Sex is such a total fantasy, so much what your society makes you believe, which is total bullshit. Oh course, in our day and age, sex sells everything. Sex is a commodity, it's no longer personal.

***

I never watched Sex in the City, but I've thought, What an abomination! How disgusting. We've lost the virtue of primitive lust, aside from everything else. There is certain purity in primitive lust that is much of what turn on is.

I'm actually talking about primitive lust in a man, because that's what brings it out in me ... *if* I like the way he does it. And how can you put that in words?

It's like the story of the lady spider who spins the web and waits for the male to approach. As he steps on the web, if the right vibrations occur she will mate with him and eat him later. But if the wrong vibrations occur, she will eat him immediately.

So men are terrified by women ... and desire them insanely. It's all nature's plan. Nature has it figured out. We are so caught by that primitive plan. Really, we think we can escape but we never do, don't you think? Both men and women, we each do our part.

I think we are all vulnerable creatures basically out looking for the same thing. And that's where we get distracted and become disgusting. The author Osho says, in his *Creativity* book, that when we want fame, power, respectability and admiration from outside sources all the time, we're screwed.

That's why us little people, who are still very creative beings, can have the joy of life not matched by anybody else. Even Bill Gates. Do you think he's happier than we are? You can have many big houses and be miserable in all of them.

I was always a rebel. For the first fourteen years of my life, I was the good girl of the family, then I became the black sheep, even with three sisters. I became the rebel first, and then I became the sexual rebel.

***

If a man loved me, that was endearing, no matter how long or how little I'd known him or been with him. Sometimes you get into it with a man and you know he doesn't love you, but maybe you're fascinated by other things.

I always want to know. When I sleep with a man, I know a lot. I know through my body who and what he is in a way I can't put into words. And that's why I seek that experience. It's about so much more than sexual ecstasy, sex is.

It's a way of communicating, not communicating, hiding, being open, being hostile, being dominant, being submissive, being receptive. You play out every role. I think the role playing is probably more profound and interesting to me than the orgasm.

I feel like in a way I've never been able to surrender enough to a man to receive total sexual ecstasy ... because I've never trusted enough. I've not trusted enough because I've been hurt and disappointed too many times, like we all have in love.

A specific trait I find endearing is a sense of humor. It's terribly important and that's the truth. A man who can make you laugh, can save most any situation.

On the other hand, domination, subtle or unsubtle, that's what kills it for me. And the older you get the sniffier you get, meaning you can sniff domination out in a minute and then you know—this ain't gonna work!

There is no one way domination looks. It just feels like slavery. Maybe it's not even that obvious. After sex or before sex, or it may have nothing to do with sex at all. Because what happens then? Are you like a stove, now you can be turned on or turned off? I like what Grace Slick said—'I'm like an 18 wheeler and you gotta go through the gears one at a time, baby.' And that extends over a lifetime—it isn't just one night or two years or whatever.

I've learned to ask myself about a man, 'What do you really mean here and what do you want? And can I trust you with my eternal soul?' I turned down the Presbyterian minister for that very reason, and that was very hot sex.

I think it's a personal thing, how each person operates. For me, the best sex is with love. That's what makes it thrilling. It's an expression of love. That's the turn on. If I don't feel that, then I'm not turned on.

Sex without love is not usually very good either, but it can be an interesting experience. You just learn more about people. The drive was there even if it wasn't fulfilled—the drive to couple.

\*\*\*

Things changed for me gradually as I got older. It wasn't overnight. You can think about sex in your 20s, 30s, 40s, 50s, 60s and all those decades are different. In my 40s, I think I was still experimenting but a little more cautious a little earlier in each relationship. And part of it—why you go out and seek the coupling—is just a certain kind of restlessness.

I think if you have sex into your 50s, you want something that means more. Me, I have been alone for a very long time. Going on a date and the thought of getting to know somebody and them getting to know me is, in a way, exhausting. I think some of the people who are dearest to me are the ones who really know me, I don't have to prove myself . . . who she is, what she is.

That takes a lot of energy and build up. You have to be ready to value that person for a long time, to give them that much time and energy. By the time you've come through your 50s and into your 60s, you're thinking about your mortality and how much time you have left.

It's like, what do you want to do with that time and energy? Do you want to waste it? You want to estimate right away 'is this worth my time here?' Because you're no longer overtaken by the sexual urge to couple unwisely or as a dalliance, or on some whimsical notion, you don't feel like you have to couple to be complete. It's all different.

You know yourself more and if you've lived alone for awhile, you know how to be with yourself. You're not overcome by that drive to complete yourself with another person, although you certainly feel it and wish you could have that ideal partner.

\*\*\*

I have the perfect answer to what I'd say to a granddaughter. Be yourself. Don't be a slave for anything or anybody. And that means to a state, organization or a man.

Everything is political. Certainly sex is. Everything is political and the only time sex is good is when you can transcend and get beyond politics. At least for me.

I think some people get off on pseudo-rape or bondage or s&m, or whatever. I really think that we can talk about sex and desire as two different things. Desire is like lightening, it hits you or it doesn't. No rhyme or reason, it's either there or not there. The collapsing quantum wave. All your past and all your future collapsing into that one wave of energy.

That alone certainly teaches you the lesson of not judging ... because it's impossible to resist. If you're struck by lightning, what possible chance do you have to resist? You're struck by lightning! You're in the throes of it. There's no resistance.

It's all political. The 'good girl'—she's the one who has been domesticated by the patriarchy. The 'bad girl' is true to her own sexual nature. That's what I think.

# 4

# Jeanne

Let's see, I probably became aware of the good girl/bad girl concept in grade school. My mom was raised in Kentucky—real church country—by one of her great aunts. They were god-fearing people and they took a bath every Saturday night. 'You can't do anything until you get married and yada yada yada.'

So my mom went with my dad for four years before they got married, when they were living in Michigan. Then my dad moved out to California to Topanga Canyon and my mom moved out shortly after that. And oh my god they were living in sin for six months before they got married. I betcha I was in my 20s, and she'd never said boo about that until I wanted to live with somebody.

She said 'you'll have to talk to your father.' She kept everything so secretive. I can remember when I was younger, if they both decided to get frisky, oh my god, you had to be so quiet and lock the bedroom door. Oh, god forbid, anybody would share anything. It was so cloistered. That's what I was raised around.

She never actually talked to me about sex. No, she figured that I would learn in junior high and high school. The only thing she told me was that you could get pregnant in like five minutes ... And don't *ever* let this happen. But she never told me how that happened—it was that closed.

Anytime I would say anything about sex she would get so tense. I finally figured she didn't know how to respond and she was just so afraid. She sort of talked to me about my period. It was a case of I got my period and then she explained to me what was happening. It was one of those things you just learn to deal with, she said.

And then when I moved away from home it was like—oh my god, I should have a shrine to God in my apartment and not do anything because I was out of her control. When I was at home she could control me, she thought, but when I moved she couldn't do anything. 'Well, I called you last night, where were you?' happened several times.

And then for awhile, when I first moved away I was like Suzy Slut. I couldn't get enough of it. I was very lucky I didn't get any diseases but I was like well . . . yeah . . . I like this! This is okay!

✳✳✳

In high school I had had to be such a good girl because there was no room to bring shame on the family. It was very clear that you don't get pregnant or become an unwed mother. They were strict. And I was an only child. No wonder I went wild when I left home.

The girls at school talked about sex but usually only if they went all the way. In a sense I was envious. Wow, I wonder what that feels like. Can you do that and not get pregnant? No way! I saw girls who got pregnant and they went away. Still, I just wanted to try it.

My dad didn't know what to do with me. He had eight brothers and one sister. So when I came along, a girl, he didn't know how to treat me. I was different. He said I should be more feminine and I said 'Dad—I can't play on the football team or the baseball team.' So I was stuck between being a tomboy and trying to be feminine.

I tried to experiment before I lost my virginity but I was always so scared. I would be so tense wanting to enjoy it, but I couldn't enjoy it. Because of my mom's background, I couldn't do it. It was just really hard for me. I bought into the fear and guilt.

Until I got on my own—then I figured what she didn't know wouldn't hurt her. What she didn't see, that type of thing—so one of the best things I could do was move away. It wasn't about what God saw . . . it was her.

I moved away when I was 20. I loved my apartment. I could have guys visit at 10 or 11 o'clock at night! That was cool! It was just nice to know there was nobody there. I could begin to relax and enjoy sex. At first it was hard for me because I was still so worked up with guilt on the inside—so I would just want to please my partner, not necessarily get pleased myself.

✳✳✳

I hardly ever had orgasms, hard as I could try. After the first one, when I did get one, I was okay but getting to that first one . . . I didn't really have orgasms for three years except when I masturbated—and never with a partner. That was really frustrating. Then my thinking about myself became, 'Okay, now you've turned into just such a whore and that's all you're worth.'

I would go out with different guys, but I wouldn't necessarily go to bed with all of them. I lived down in LA for five years where I met a couple of guys and one of them wanted to marry me and of course I didn't love him. It was real hard for me at that time to express myself, to put my emotions out.

So if somebody would ask me to do something, I'd say 'Yeah, fine,' but my heart wouldn't be into it. I just did it because I wanted to be liked and that's why after awhile I thought of myself as a whore because I did it for people to like me and not for what I really was.

It took the first two years when I lived down in LA before I got over the good girl/bad girl thing, when I knew for sure no one was going to call my mom. Then that bad girl took over. Still, it always seemed like it was rushed. I just wanted to get liked, I just wanted people's approval. It didn't matter about my feelings.

I really thought in those terms. It had become my morality because my mom had ingrained it in me. When I left home I learned I didn't have to be a goody two shoes anymore. With me being an only child and a girl, I was really protected and sheltered. That's what really screwed me up, as I learned later on in life. I tried to talk to my mom about it once, not to be mad, but just to let her know. Well, we know where this conversation went … why do I even bother to open up my mouth?

***

Over the years I did learn to respect myself. But when I was first married my husband always wanted to do it once or twice *every* night. When you're not used to that … well, I said let's go a little slow. And he said 'You don't love me—it's natural and you should be sexual so you must not love me.'

So again I would give in because I wanted him to like me, but damn, I was so tired all the time. I finally figured maybe I didn't want that much sex. Then it got to the point where I lost interest because it felt like he was forcing me. I mean I like sex but every flippin' night?

Finally we sat down and talked about it. I said 'Not every night.' He said 'I have a very high libido.' I said 'You better learn how to compromise that libido. We can work out some kind of agreement. I don't mean limited to Saturday night—not any set time but I can't do it every night.' See, for the first five years he wasn't working, so it was my salary that was coming in and that made a difference.

I think he probably was a good lover—just not to me. Everything we did was for him to get off. No tenderness, no emotion. Foreplay was, 'Brace yourself!' It just didn't go anywhere for me. I put up with it for years because I didn't want to 'lose my man.' We were married for twenty-three years.

I did play around on him, but it wasn't until the last couple years of his life. He was ill and there was so sex. He was on oxygen 24 hours a day. I was so afraid I was going to break him or crush him. And it wasn't an appealing sight, I was honest with him. I'm sorry, this is where I am. I'd give him hugs and kisses and I was affectionate towards him but sex was nonexistent. It had been for awhile, probably a year and half before he got sick. So then it was pretty close to seven years without sex when he died—a long time.

Then this gentleman came, a really good friend, and I used to go out and cry on his shoulder. I'd get so frustrated when things were rough. And it just happened between us, no one planned it. If my husband ever knew he never said anything, which he would have. I felt guilty for all of about 10 seconds.

***

The idea of virginity and monogamy may have some intrinsic value for some women. Maybe even for women in general there is a point to it. Not for me.

Some women have chosen to live their lives as the good girl—virgin until you get married. But that wasn't for me because I wanted to know. How do you know if there's going to be good sex if you don't try it out? What happens if you're not compatible? So I figured let's try it out way before we get married. I didn't want to get married. He's the one who wanted to. We lived together for 11 years before I would marry him.

Virginity means something different to different people. Like in India and a lot of other places, some people cloister their daughters away and they still have the arranged marriages. Some kill their daughters if they have sex. If you couldn't go home and you couldn't get married, what do you do? If a woman is raped, she is stoned to death for being raped. Those are beliefs out there in the world.

***

I experienced a sexual awakening not too many years ago. Oh, yeah! There was a young gentleman who was 29 at the time. I was 53. He was just a really good friend who stopped by to say hello to my new cats. We sat down, had a glass of wine and maybe I had one too many glasses of wine. In any event, we ended up in bed.

It was a true awakening for me. Oh my god—I couldn't believe what this dude could do. I didn't know you could do that, feel that way. He was all tenderness—the attention was all about me, about pleasing me, into me. I just threw caution to the wind and I went for it. It was the most perfect time.

When we were done, I had been wowed! 'Thank you so much for waking me up.' I said to him. 'Now I know I can do better than the guys I've been going out with, I can be satisfied and I deserve what just happened.' It was a deep revelation to me.

A couple of weeks later, it was Valentine's Day, he stopped by again. I told him that I couldn't put into words what he had done for me but thank you. I knew it'd never happen again, I was okay with that. I was so thankful for this one time. He just looked at me.

'You really mean that, don't you?' he asked. I said yeah. 'It's like a whole new world now. Like it's okay to be me. If someone calls and I don't want to see them, it's fine. I don't need them to like me just because they want to come over. I don't have to do it anymore. If somebody comes over, that doesn't mean it's going to happen. I can control the shots now. Yeah, Baby!

I still see him—he'll stop by for a glass of wine. There's no tension—it's just a real comfortable friendship.

We decided—I think it was mostly me—about the age difference—that we wouldn't do it again. 'You're old enough to be his mom,' I told myself and that tripped me out. It was just something that happened—that situation, those circumstances. I could have said no, but I'd of kicked myself the rest of my life ... or I wouldn't have known what I'd missed.

What changed for me was that I had multiple orgasms. It was like an earthquake going through my body. I thought, God Jeanne, you've really missed a lot. I focused on the situation at hand and it all changed. I was allowing myself to drop all those walls and barriers and really just give myself to him—not worrying about if he was going to be satisfied. It was being selfish and it was a 'me' thing. Yet look what I got back. I still have the friendship intact and look at how much he got back too.

The whole experience has carried over—it's made such a difference in my life. I've been seeing a couple of gentleman who had to realize I'm not a trained seal. If he knocks on the back door and says 'I only have 15-20 minutes, let's ...' that's just not going to happen anymore. I guess I'm not as needy as I was. If another gentleman calls and I'm not in mood, I just say no. Before I would let him come over. Now, I have this whole new world view.

The quality of my self-pleasuring, masturbation, has changed too. Now, I don't have that restrictive thing I had put in my own mind. It's okay to enjoy sex, to pleasure myself. But see, it took so many years to get rid of that stigma because it was so firmly embedded in my brain.

It was a combination of good girl/bad girl concepts and self-esteem. I believed the only reason someone wanted to come over was to fuck me but I was so caught up in wanting people to like me—their approval—which stems from the good girl/bad girl thing. It carried on throughout my life. Some people said 'You should have gotten rid of him a long time ago.' Well—coulda, woulda, shoulda. But if you don't know ... and if you ask questions, well, then you're a slut.

If you ask questions about sex—well, why do you need to know? Are you having sex? Are you a slut? My mom—I can still hear her voice whispering around my brain. I thought she was going to have a heart attack when she took me to OB-GYN to get birth control pills. I was nineteen. I went with my mom because at that time you couldn't get them without one of your parents with you. That's the way Ventura was in the 60s. I lost my virginity when I was nineteen. I had tried so hard before then, but ...

***

I liked sex before my awakening—it's a natural part of life—but when it gets derailed, sometimes you have to play catch up. Now, it's good to call the shots myself. I still don't like it every night.

The good thing is, my sex drive is at an all time high of an 8-9 (out of 10) right now. It's gone from a 1-2 at the end of my marriage to 8-9 now. It's definitely grown with age for me.

It's been a slow process, over the course of the last ten years. Now I've gone from a whore to a slut—things are definitely looking up! I think I've gotten a much higher sex drive since menopause. Some nights I'm a ghost-buster—who am I going to call tonight?

I'm definitely still sexually active and I intend to stay that way, ever since I got that hysterectomy when I was 43. Reason was, I had three miscarriages, bleeding, pills, endometriosis and chronic pelvic pain.

No more Advil, cramps, no worries, no getting pregnant, no diseases. Hey, yeah! I'd be in bed for three weeks out of every month. It was ridiculous. Once I knew that I couldn't get pregnant, I wouldn't have to go through another miscarriage ... it made a difference.

***

An endearing lover, to me, is someone who is gentle ... tender ... who can last a little while ... who knows about my body as well as his own body. If somebody can take me through a couple of orgasms before intercourse, then, hopefully we can come together. If that happens, it's great—there's just something about coming together that's really special to me. My two orgasms have to happen before he gets off because usually once he's done, he's done.

Tenderness and gentleness are endearing. Someone who, if I do some-thing wrong, tells me nicely, isn't a real prick about it. I want a nice experience, gentle, so when we're done we lay back on the bed and my whole body is glowing and tingling. And afterwards, he takes hold of my hand, puts a leg over me so we can just be one for a little while. Sometimes, I don't get up and take a shower right away because I still have his scent on me and I like that.

The most annoying habit of a lover is a guy who just flippin' rushes through it. It's not a race here, folks. I want to make love with someone, I don't want to fuck him. It's defeating the purpose. I don't even get a sweat up before, oh you're done? Excuse me while I move on.

It's annoying if they fart. I hate that. If you're laying there and here's this real nice tender moment and all of sudden he lets one rip, couldn't you at least go to the bathroom for that?

I'm not really into the kinky stuff like s&m. I would try it maybe once just to see what it would be like. I won't get up on stage and make love in front of a whole bunch of people—I'm real private. But if it sounds okay, I'd try it and I might not like it. There's nothing inherently wrong or bad in sex.

Like where do you have your best orgasm—the clit or the vagina? How can one be bad? I think it depends on the person you're with. Somebody can touch you on the arm and that can get you going. It doesn't matter—caress on your cheek or breast. It's not a particular place. It depends on the person.

The best characteristic of a good lover, I think, is the way he accepts you and your body. Some guys are boob people, or knees, or feet. What's important is, 'What can I do to get you excited?' It's the energy you can pull off of them. Some men know exactly what to do and some don't. You don't want to be rude to them, but where did you learn? Clueless. I think it depends on the woman who trains him.

***

I would like to say to younger women, 'Don't be so quick to give yourself away. I'm not saying stay a virgin, but don't fall into the trap I did, thinking that if you screw someone they're going to like you. Don't be so hasty to give yourself away'.

As far as good girl/bad girl issues are concerned, I think no matter what anybody says, it's something that each woman has to find out for herself—because every woman is different, every mom is different. My mom said, 'You have to be a good girl.' Somebody else's mom could say, 'You should be good and here are the reasons why.'

What's good for me isn't necessarily good for you … or bad. Everybody's different. It's time they lifted some of these old categorized sayings, like you have to be a virgin until you get married—they probably weren't. Your skirt is too short … your pants are too tight …

We tell a little girl what not to do, within this box of what's acceptable. And then all of a sudden, as a young woman, she can think outside that box—that's what happened to us. There's a whole different world out there. It's not at all what they told us.

# 5

# Lyla

I never heard anybody talking to me about good girls and bad girls—sexually—although in the convent school I went to for high school, one of the nuns played tapes of unwed mothers talking about being unwed and having children. The nun never said anything about the tapes ahead of time, she just put them on. She probably wasn't allowed to but did it anyhow. Remember, this was before birth control pills came along.

I was such a tomboy. I didn't think about sex early on and only slowly gleaned what it was all about. I remember summer camp between 8$^{th}$ and 9$^{th}$ grade. The other girls would talk about the top of beer bottles—kind of crude—that was the first time I understood about the shape of the male member.

I couldn't be dictated to about morality—it's one of the things I most appreciate about my strong Catholic upbringing—mostly my mother's influence. She taught us to think for ourselves.

I knew I would decide when I would lose my virginity. I didn't worry about being taken. I'd decided it would happen at the end of high school.

I did fantasize about men's bodies, usually down in the Grotto where we had morning Mass. It was quiet there and I felt safe enough to think about this stuff. I fantasized more about the shape and form of a man's body, not so much the juicy stuff—the actually doing of the deed. I guess I was an intellectual.

I became sexually active at seventeen. My father talked to us four girls about our curfew—boy, we really didn't look forward to reckoning with my father about coming home after our curfew. Many times he had made the comment 'you are responsible for your own sins' and he hoped we would graduate high school before becoming sexually active. And 'when you start, you're on your own,' he always said. It's all related in my mind to not missing our curfew...

Another positive advantage of being at a Catholic school—someone (of us students) was always making fun of something they (the nuns and priests) were trying to incorporate into us. For instance, the nuns said French kissing was a sin and we knew that was bunk. It was fun and didn't feel sinful at all to us, so we laughed about it.

If you were dating a boy at a Catholic school, you knew he had a range of life expanding information and experience beyond the school. I knew the priests were feeding them information like the nuns were feeding us. But the boys, and us girls, knew life was wholesome, so the idea of sex being a deadly sin just wasn't getting through.

My feeling was that I was privileged to get sex in the future and being told by my father that it was my responsibility made me more open. Our generation wasn't going to wait until we were married to make love, although I grew up very close to that slightly older generation who still bought that stuff.

I remember heavy petting sessions in the kitchen while my boyfriend was tutoring me in math and we'd just get squirrelly all over each other. Of course, my father was out in the living room ... we never considered going any further. Ha!

I'd been keeping this guy waiting for two years and when we finally had sex during the summer after graduation, of course it was wonderful.

\*\*\*

Actually the first time I ever felt like a 'bad girl' was after I'd moved to British Columbia. I used to go over to a friend's apartment and listen to music. They were musicians. One time I had just met this guy but there was immediate chemistry between us. I knew it would be a one night stand but I didn't know who he was or if he was clean. I was just having sex for the sake of sex after ending a two year relationship with my boyfriend.

The outcome was that he was too big to get inside me. It was the first time I ever experienced an unsuccessful sexual encounter. We were both willing but he was just too big, he couldn't get inside me.

That happened to me one other time too, years and years later. There were no moral issues involved but he was so big, he had to have had problems with women all his life. In both cases I think we each had adult responses, talking to each other and staying friends.

\*\*\*

When I was twenty-three I had an abortion. I felt bad about it but it was my personal experience, not some moral issue. I was having such a really hard time putting myself through school that I knew I couldn't do a child. It took me years before I talked about it at all and I still don't talk about it much. Really, I think I feel most remorse about not telling the father about the baby before the abortion.

I didn't let others judge me, only God. But see, God is benevolent—I really knew that—so I didn't need to even think about other people judging me.

What's changed for me now, at sixty years old, is that I really do believe these are the golden years. I'm still able and I want to have sex but I'm in a different head space. I've always seen sex as wholesome and I've never had much curiosity or need for lust. But several times over the years I've gone into the head space about who I am. What is sex at my age? I'm no longer who I was ... except that I still don't care what anyone else thinks.

I've gone back to the time when I was a sexual unknown, when I was a virgin. My reactions, my involvement is unknown to me, as well as to a potential partner. Now if I open my legs, it will be because of a big overwhelming energy. It will be a wet and juicy ride that we take together, different from when you have to work at it.

It's always been a mystery to me about why sometimes you have to work at it and sometimes you don't. Is it fate? Is it chemistry? Paths of energy that cause yes to this one and no to that one? I really want it to be special every time. I don't worry about whether I'm still sexual ... yet.

\*\*\*

What else has changed? I've always been pretty open about sex, wanting to both get into it and be overwhelmed by it—although those two things are actually the same thing. To me it's really about the right guy. If it seems impersonal ... well, actually I don't do that anymore—being turned on for the sake of being turned on, without the relationship.

I've always been orgasmic and juicy and experienced multiple orgasms. Well, in the last ten years there haven't been so many multiples. I don't have the same reserves anymore. I have no interest in going all night in one wild session and I don't just fuck for the sake of fucking.

Men should have this personal connection thing, like 'have you ever really fallen in love?' Those are interesting stories men should be able to tell. Some men seem to have reverence for women and some don't. I remember one man I had a really good relationship with until I got in bed with him ... and then I ended the relationship.

I want to dance with a lover first. I want to feel how he responds to me, to my body, out on a dance floor. How is he going to treat me? Still, you can't always tell ahead of time what kind of lover a guy will be.

***

If I have any advice or wisdom now, especially for younger girls and women, I would say, if you find someone who is really special to you, try to set life aside. I mean, have your eyes wide open about life but set it aside and don't let it interfere with you and that someone really special. For instance, if you find yourself as the wiser one and understand that you need to give him sexual advice, then do that. It's a gift to yourself. You won't know who you are in ten years until you get there.

Watch yourself in your own desires and particularly in what you want from a male. Watch yourself as much as you watch him. Sometimes that isn't an easy road so you have to have compassion for yourself. It isn't vanity—you need to think about these things, contemplate them, and meditate on them.

A turning point for me was when I learned that I could deliberately excite a male—like with oral sex. That's when I understood that if he couldn't get it up, I could do something about it. Of course, I always assume that if I manipulate something, there will be a price to pay. But if he can't get it up and really wants to, it's an artful thing to know how to help him.

Talking about what I want or like … hmmm. If he spends lots of time on my breasts, I am much more turned on. The vagina to me is the sacred mystery. I want him to grow into it, through smell and the play between our responses to each other. I really don't appreciate it when a man goes right down on me. Like I said, I want to dance first, see his response to me as a person first.

That sacred mystery stuff is not because he is rubbing on my clit. It happens before he's even touching me. It's like the right kiss can go everywhere in my body—now that's a sacred mystery!

Yes, I masturbate but I'm not big at it. It always reflects what's going on in my head. Masturbating usually makes me feel lonely. I like to feel where I'm at but I don't want to take masturbation to great depths. I don't really want to analyze myself that much.

I still have sexual dreams and jump around all over my bed. In the shower I check out myself and take a nice little journey, you know, check that it still feels soft and really rich to me.

One bad experience I had, I needed a biopsy of my cervix. The doctor told me to breath really deep while she took two scrapes on the uterus lining. It was a painful but necessary preventative step. I really didn't like those stirrups—the experience was physically difficult and traumatic. The doctor, though, she was wonderful.

I guess I've never had any problems connecting with either the wonderful wholesomeness of sex or the pain of a pap smear.

I figure it's just me and God and the guy, in sex. I always learn while I'm doing it. It's not an experiment, but rather a journey. I've always felt very trustful. Even though I know stuff goes wrong and evil happens, it happens over there somewhere.

***

Good girl, bad girl? Definitely there are both but I think it's how girls get involved. The saucier they try to be, the more it leads to that impersonal stuff. It could be like Dante's inferno—people paying no attention to their own values—cheap sex, chasing dollars, chasing after having a partner, tearing your hair out.

Bad *and* good girls can also be light hearted—it doesn't have to be nasty. It's really about our own willingness to be intimate and that's a judgment we put on ourselves.

# 6

# Carla

I'm 58 years old and I've had adventures. Even though I was married, I had lots of adventures. I've never been the *good girl* like we thought in the 60s, when we were in high school.

With all the wonderful people there are in the world why would you ever want to be with just one person? So here and there I would have lots and lots of one night stands. I guess you'd call it cheating on your husband. For me, I just stayed in the moment ... you know, if the opportunity presented itself, I went for it.

I was raised Catholic. You didn't do 'it' if you were a good Catholic girl. In fact, though, in high school in my hometown in Colorado I remember some wonderful experiences when I was learning about making out.

But never ever would you go all the way. No. And, it was not okay to let the boys fondle your breasts. One could be sticking his hands up my shirt ... well, it was just *no*. You could kiss and kiss, my god, and just get so hot and so excited but then, absolutely not any more than that. Never. You'd be screwed. Your reputation would be ruined. You'd be a whore.

Well, I allowed them to touch my breasts. But then you had to stop them ... and yourself! You just had to stop. There was to be no sex before marriage, period, all the way through high school and on into college.

\*\*\*

I can remember the first guy who just absolutely refused to take my no, no, no. He just didn't pay any attention to me. I was completely frightened afterward that I was pregnant and I was only in my second month in college.

I was in a play and this guy wanted to walk me home. All the other guys, if I said no to them, they would stop. I mean they might make another few feeble attempts and then they'd stop. But this guy did not listen. He started taking my clothes off as soon as we got up to his apartment but he was literally pushing me along. Not forcefully and not meanly, really, but just completely unrelenting in his pressure even though all the time I'm saying 'no, no, don't, don't.' He just kept going until we had sex.

Yes, I felt like I'd been raped. It was not pleasant at all. I did not like it at all. But at that time, you didn't think about it as rape. It was my first time. Later I had no guilt, nor did I feel bad. I didn't hate him or anything—although I was pretty scared of him. I tried not to see him again.

I even remember his name. Mostly I was scared I was pregnant, and as soon as my period started, I forgot about the whole thing. At the time, I felt like I had no power. My sense of my own power was not very good. I couldn't say no effectively and they'd figure it meant 'yes yes.'

He did try it one other time. He showed up at the door and said, 'I'm going to Viet Nam. I've been drafted and I just wanted to come by and say goodbye.' It didn't really mean anything to me then. I knew about the war as we had already started protesting, but personally I was pretty relieved he was leaving, getting the hell out of my life and I wouldn't have to run into him. There was something about him after that first experience, you know ... we didn't have sex again.

***

After that, in my sexual awakening, there were two guys that I played a little game with during my freshman year. After awhile though I settled down with James as my boyfriend. He wrote me a beautiful love letter, the most beautiful thing I'd ever read, so I became his girlfriend and I stayed his girlfriend until we got married.

After we'd been married for about two years, I just wasn't sexually turned on to him anymore. Now I'm sure this was out of sheer ignorance on my part, not knowing how to work on any relationship issues, or how to talk about anything important ... like what I wanted.

It was basically kiss, and then I was supposed to be turned on and then we'd have sex and it would be wonderful. I liked it and everything. But it was all dependent on my being turned on. You know that wonderful incredible turned on passion? After my son was born, it just wasn't happening for me anymore. I interpreted that to mean that we weren't in love anymore.

I was pretty innocent, never having a mom or dad. I just didn't know anything about it.

***

We were living at the Hot Springs and this friend had read a book about couples living all together in a house, I think it was called the *Harrod Experiment*. There were three couples with their families in the book and they agreed that they could switch around and be a larger family.

Well, I just loved this idea. So one night we were at a party up the road and we decided to put this idea into practice. There were two other couples in these little cabins at the Hot Springs and we decided to start by one of us going over there and one coming here. So one night Larry would come over to my bed and James would go over with Barbara. We decided ahead of time and planned who would go where. This little experiment went on for about a month.

I remember that time with the most wonderful feeling. There were a whole bunch of us, thirty-five people and all of us friends. Some of us were coupled off, but it didn't matter because we were all friends.

It was a great freedom to me that I could look at another person, who was somebody else's husband, and I could have sexual feelings about this person and it was okay. We could go ahead and make love and it would be okay because the other partners knew about it and were involved. We weren't cheating, off on some affair—that was very much frowned on by the group.

The idea of it being all in the open seemed really wonderful to me.

***

In the end, though, I left my husband and went off with Michael for a brief time, almost eight months. All kinds of amazing stuff was happening that year—1970. I went running off to Canada with Michael and my tiny baby. I ended up going back to James, because halfway across Canada I realized I'd made a big mistake, that I needed to go back and be married and be a mother.

I was writing passionate love letters to James and he was writing them to me while I was with Michael. At the same time I was telling Michael that at the end of all this fun I was returning to my husband. Sounds weird but it was fun. We were having great sex.

When I got back here, James was occupied with starting a natural food store because he had been bitten by that bug. He had no interest in me or the baby. When we came back, he showed me no affection and was really pretty pissed at me for what I'd done.

I was attempting to settle down and figure out what was happening when all of a sudden Michael showed up. He'd stayed back in New York for a month while he was writing all sorts of passionate letters. With James's lack of interest and Michael's excess of interest, I went with Michael. By then . . . well, I was with him for more than twenty years.

\*\*\*

I was mostly monogamous . . . kind of. I had one affair with a woman who was bisexual, which I hadn't known about before. They had all these x-rated Halloween parties way back in the early 70s. She and her husband had a house that was renowned for this sort of thing.

One night Michael was gone somewhere. It was my birthday and Mary and Sam said 'We want you to spend the night tonight.' So I said okay and I loved it. It was wonderful because I was really into experimenting.

For me, it was a lark. Later though she wrote love letters and we had an affair. She was the only affair I've ever had with a woman and it really became a pain in the ass.

I made the mistake of telling Michael, thinking he would be excited about it because she was a woman. But it turned out he'd always wanted to have an affair with her, and because we couldn't all be together, he made my life miserable and I had to sneak around.

She was writing more and more of those love letters. Finally I had to lay my cards on the table and say that I just didn't feel about her the way she felt about me.

And the whole girl sex thing? In the beginning, it was trippy. Ooh, a girl. Wow. Like with anybody it was new, but I didn't like it much after two or three times. That was enough, because I'm not basically lesbian.

James and I had had this ménage-a-trois thing going at the Hot Springs, but that girl and I didn't have anything to do with each other so it wasn't a real trio.

I was willing to give it a try. Sometimes when I masturbated I'd have sexual fantasies about women. But, it was just a period of my life that faded away. I never had threesomes again. Michael was very strange. He hated it but I don't know why.

\*\*\*

While I was married to Michael, I'd go off on camping trips with a girlfriend to Mexico, even after I'd had my kids. There would always be some guys around, drinking and smoking and pretty soon somebody would start kissing me and I would just go with it. This was before AIDS of course, and all the other bad stuff so I'd just go with what felt good in the moment.

If I liked somebody or if they were a really good lover, a one night stand was the most wonderful thing. There's no commitment, it's just pure sex. When I look back on it, really, I was falling in love with each one of these guys. Love and sex were the same thing to me then . . . maybe because of the Catholic upbringing. Because I would never have had wonderful intercourse with someone I didn't like—I was a good girl!

I loved these guys. I fell in love with each and every one of them. The next day I would want to somehow keep on seeing them. Even though I knew I couldn't, I wanted to. I would think about them for days afterward. I really had feelings for them. All of them.

There was the time Michael and I split up, one of the five times, and I went down to Puerto Vallarta to live on the beach. I was playing a big romance with Juan. If he had asked me, I was completely willing to stay, to become a Mexican peasant woman with him. I was nuts, totally!

***

Honestly I do consider myself one of the bad girls. And, at the same time, I've been true to myself through all of it.

For instance, I had a major crush on my boss for years, until he got married. I knew he went to the nude beach and I showed up one Saturday. We didn't really go there together, but he did give me a ride home. Pathetic, huh?

I did do one thing—see how bad a girl I am? I love this to this day! In the beginning few years, he would open the mail. He would say come on in and bring your pad (I did shorthand in those days) and he would go through the mail and dictate letters.

I concocted a plan to send him an anonymous love letter, saying 'I love you,' so I could watch him open that letter. And that's what I did. It was great! He was just flabbergasted. I recognized the envelope when it came through. Then he looked at me when he opened it up, and quickly shut it. It definitely flustered him. I had been very careful, getting one of these blank cards so there was nothing that he could tie to me and then I completely disguised the handwriting.

***

Personally I see it as so difficult because most of the guys I meet I'm not interested in. I see younger guys that interest me. We understand and accept that whole thing with men and younger women. It's okay for an old guy to have a young woman, especially if he has money. The older woman and the younger guy, that's also okay when she has the money.

I guess I have actually been a bad girl for sure. My first husband's good little 13 year old brother—we did it. I was his very first and it was the most amazing beautiful experience. He thanked me and thanked me. He was a very advanced 13 years old. I was maybe 21 or 22. His parents were two steps away in the main house. So you think that's the bad girl?

About 1991, my son had a half cousin in town, kind of part of the family, who had a friend my son's age, 17. The friend was Korean and Caucasian and a very odd kid. He started showing up here at the house and he would hang out in the kitchen with me. "Oh, little momma. Oh mom, I like you" he would say. I can't remember the incident when all of a sudden I was turned on by him. We started kissing in the kitchen when the kids were in the living room. And he was like this little boy. Oh, it was very bad.

I wanted to have sex with him but he chickened out in the end and wouldn't go for it. I felt this passion thing until I was the one pursuing him. Goodness it was very dangerous and very bad. I was a bad girl that time.

***

I was always pushing the envelope. What I consider real bad is the strange stuff like sado-masochism ... that's bad and doesn't turn me on at all.

Or swinging. That kind of stuff was always beyond my boundaries. Even when we did trade partners, there wasn't a bunch of people all in the same room or all at the same house. He would go there and someone else would come to me. Just couples swapping.

That other stuff, like those Halloween parties that my friends had that were x-rated? At the time I didn't know what x-rated meant, I just didn't know. I've never been to an orgy and I've never wanted to.

***

As soon as I got to college, I gave up the Catholic idea of good girl/bad girl and never let it back in. I discarded Catholicism totally. Then I took on existentialism as well as sex, boys and politics. I never again saw any value in calling myself a good girl or a bad girl.

I'm just now learning that sex is, or can be, a woman's power base. Like the other day, now that I'm not supporting Fred (my last partner) in any way, he has dropped off the radar. However, he called to wish me happy Valentine's Day and to say that he loved me. And of course he called me at work where I couldn't talk to him, which really annoyed me because I couldn't say anything,

He's got a primal energy about him that is very attractive to me. I also realize that he's just completely, well ... crazy.

At the end of that phone conversation, I was glad he'd called—it made me feel good. But as the night came on and I got home, I never even thought to call him back. I almost wrote him a note. I got all the way to having a paper and pen in front of me and then I said nope. Nope.

I've always just given myself away. Just given me away to whoever asked. The minute I felt attracted to somebody, I just gave myself away. I gave my sexual energy away that way too. But no more.

If Fred wasn't so messed up with intimacy issues, we could have had some hot sex. I thought I adored him. Who knows, though? The kind of sex that I want now is slow and intimate.

***

I don't like blow jobs, I don't like rough sex, I don't like what you see on the movies. That's not the kind of sex I like. I like *just barely there*. I was coming on that way with Fred, but realized right away he wasn't going to like that. He was rougher than James.

I just kept hoping that somehow, somewhere, he would be like I wanted him to be. I was so nuts about him. Anyway... It's been quite a while, years, since I changed into wanting slow and easy sex.

However, when I look at normal guys my age, they don't do anything for me. I know it's about getting to know somebody and all that... but just on a physical level, I rarely see ... every once in a while ... one who looks interesting to me. Interesting and sane. Rarely.

Now I'm very comfortable being celibate. I'm not sexually wanting a man so much that just anyone is okay ... just wanting it, to the point where I'd be out hoping to score? Just for that? No, I don't need to do that anymore.

I self-pleasure maybe once every two weeks, especially if I smoke pot. Pot is like a huge aphrodisiac for me. I do have a favorite fantasy but I'm not going to tell you what it is.

***

There was an incident that I look back on and say 'that was the best.' It was a time with Michael when we were traveling down from San Francisco and he had hurt his back. That's part of my favorite fantasy, someone that's really vulnerable. I love that, especially when we're both vulnerable.

So we were staying in some podunk town driving down the coast and "Gorillas in the Mist" was playing on the tv. We made love to the entire movie and we never saw it at all but it was always in the background. And I think that was probably the best. Out of this world and we were out of our minds. It was like meditation, it was so far beyond ordinary sex. The best.

There was another time, with a guy who showed up in my life. He was the most expert lover that I have ever had. He had this knowledge of a woman's body and did amazing things that made me feel wonderful, coming and coming and coming. He knew where to touch me and he was a friend. That was pretty good.

A lot of those one night stand things were pretty great too. I can't remember any that weren't. I never had any bad sexual experiences, ever.

Except that one guy who gave me crabs. That was the worst. He was so sweet, too. When I drove him back to his car, he reaches into the back and says 'Here, I want you to have these' and hands me some stereo speakers. When I got home Michael said, 'Where the hell did these come from?'

Oh, and there was one other brief funny thing. Michael and I would talk about how he was very young (I was 24 and he was only 20) and I was his first big relationship. He was always with me. I robbed him from the cradle and he'd never gotten experience from any other relationships.

So this one time, when he had a crush on a woman and he came and told me, I told him to go and do it. So he did—had a weekend with his fling. It made me feel kind of funny and quite excited at the same time. I wasn't jealous. It brought back memories of those old days of switching and swapping.

***

Lovers absolutely have to be the most excellent kissers. And none of this sticking your tongue way down in my throat like that ... at least not in the beginning.

I'm sure it's all very nice to have candles and incense and stuff but that's never seemed very important to me. I don't need a lot of fluff.

It's got more to do with the connection, the care—no quick moves. Michael and I made love hundreds of time. It wasn't always the most excellent, but he always wanted to be sure that I came. That was one of his big deals. He would always always help me come, he would masturbate me. And we did the timing birth control thing so he would pull out and work it perfectly for him.

It kind of screwed up my coming, so then he would always help me come. I always thought that was really nice. Whereas Fred could've given a shit about me coming.

***

So what's most endearing? Caring about if I'm having a good time. Talking to me.

What's so annoying is when there is no intimacy. I always felt intimacy with those one night stands, whereas with Fred I never ever felt intimate.

Intimacy, to me, feels like when we're becoming one ... dropping all our defenses and boundaries and just blending and melting into each other ... feeling whatever we want to feel.

And not having to think or wonder about whether I am giving him a good enough blow job, like with Fred. Or even if I *can* give him a good enough blowjob.

I was so excited sometimes by the fact that we were actually making love, with James, but it wasn't working. It was only in the first two years when I was so hot for him and then after that my excitement went away.

All I have to do is think of Fred to be annoyed—how he makes love, just expecting me to be a piece of property for his pleasure. Like, 'Okay, give me a blow job. Here I am, just take care of me' kind of thing. It was like being a prostitute. For the little while that we actually did have a sex life, there were a couple of times in the beginning that were kind of nice.

There was a time, after almost a year together, when we were making love every couple of weeks. I'd come in from the bathroom and he'd have all the candles lit and he'd be laying out flat and then I would know this was it, time to give him a blow job. He'd say 'Honey, I think there's some of that magic oil over there.' I would go get the jojoba oil for a hand job. It was all about getting him warmed up. It's like you'd have to rev him up.

I guess that's what he thought women are supposed to do. Maybe he learned it from the prostitutes in Viet Nam. They were all so young. He was a little boy over there and that's where he learned what he thought he was supposed to do sexually and what a woman was supposed to do.

That's also what our mothers did. If you were married, you satisfied your husband. Our mothers would just lay there, on their backs, performing.

So those are the most annoying of lovers' habits—the lack of intimacy and the expectation and entitlement attitude.

***

I guess I've never really given sex that much thought as something you can learn about. I don't think about it too much now either. Except when I was with Fred and not getting any—then I really thought about it.

What I'm trying to say is that I'm not one of those people who decorates her house to make it like a love nest. I never felt that I was really a super sensual person. I've got my foot in the door but I'm not overly that way. In some ways I kind of wish I was—because I think that would be pretty fun too.

Like studying Tantric yoga and listening to tapes on how to achieve higher orgasms. Deliberately putting a lot of energy and effort into it. I don't do that.

It always just came to me—hormones and such. We were young and hormones were working great and our whole focus was boys so I felt like I was an average healthy kind of a girl.

***

So what's average and healthy for people our age? I have no idea. I've never really thought about it. I think it depends on your health and I would imagine it depends on how you've lived your life. Like a person who has been sort of asexual, certainly at this point will continue on that way. And someone who's always been interested, if they're still healthy and have some libido left, will still be interested.

In our society, the good girl doesn't acknowledge her sexual nature and the bad girl does. It's all very Catholic. You still hear men talk about marrying the good girl, even though now nine year olds dress up like little sluts.

Have you been down State Street late at night? Everybody's walking around with skirts up to here, and it all looks like their underwear. They say it's just the look, but I don't believe putting nine year old girls in bikinis is authentically celebrating feminine energy. It's actually patronizing to feminine energy.

It's exactly the same as it's always been. Good girl. It's really gone underground, it wouldn't be hip to be talking this way, but there's still a boundary. If you step over that, you're not safe. You're subject to ridicule.

Like Madonna. Or movies like "Wild At Heart" with Laura Dern and Nicholas Cage. She is fabulous—the archetypal bad girl. She took off with the bad boy and they just raised hell. Then they came to a very bad end.

In the movies, do the bad girls ever get to go off into the sunset or do they always meet some misfortune? I think they still get punished—unless some white knight comes along and she's rescued, like in "Pretty Girl." Not many years ago there was still the underlying feeling that if a woman got raped, she did something to bring it on herself.

I think that down deep inside it's still the same. A highly sexual woman is chastised and put down for it. It's not appropriate to be highly sexual. Those are the social sanctions today.

\*\*\*

I figure I've had a pretty cool sex life. I had a lot of adventures, even including Fred. I don't have any regrets. While I don't know what's coming next, I also don't feel that I'll never have sex again. I'm open for whatever happens.

I can see it as a lovely thing—I would meet a lovely man who had his own place and was very comfortable living by himself. Every once in a while we would go out. At this point, I have zero interest in having a live-in relationship with somebody because I've just been burned too many times.

Part of it is me—I had no models for a good relationship. I grew up with an old-maid aunt. At eleven years old, I went to live with my dad and stepmother who turned out to be an alcoholic who ran off on binges all the time. I didn't learn how to do the ebb and flow or whatever it is that you have to know about relationships.

I go into them with 'I love you, I love you, I love you' as my mantra. But nobody can love me as much as I want to be loved, so then we get into troubles.

It's not easy for me or maybe I've just never found the right fit. It's almost like the little kid's book <u>Are You My Mother?</u> That's what it was like for me—'Are you my lover?' 'Are you my husband?' If I had good feelings, then I'd think 'Oh, you must be the one' and I would never think about money or personality or values. I never gave any of that a passing thought—it was all just the sexual chemistry for me.

Anyway, I've had a good sex life. Maybe I'm not in the 100 club, but in the 30s at least.

***

Thinking about what I would tell my granddaughters about sex? My first thought is, get as much as you can. But then it is so dangerous now. It's different because you can't be as free, innocent, like I was very innocent. Well, maybe you can.

So maybe what I would say is, just be sure to enjoy it. Always enjoy it, don't have any sort of guilt. If it feels good, it is good. I guess that's it. Can the guilt. If it feels good, it is good. Many people feel guilty when it feels good. In the old days, when it felt good, it must be bad and you must be one of the bad girls if you liked it.

That was the thing—if a woman liked it. In my grandmother's time, if you liked it, there was something wrong with you. *You were not supposed to enjoy it.* My aunt would say that she would sneak in to listen to her mom talking with her friends around the kitchen table and they always talked about how horrible, how painful sex was. They would never ever admit that they liked it. That was the Victorian women of just two generations ago.

***

I've been true to myself—I enjoyed it when I could get it. Now I'm still true to myself because I'm not willing to compromise on either having a relationship in order to have sex, or on having sex without having an authentic relationship. I guess I've been a bad girl and a good girl.

# 7

# Annie Laurie

That name comes from my grandmother, from a song she knew, I think.
I'm from New Zealand and the whole good girl/bad girl thing was most
definitely in my life.

I was raised Catholic and we went to church every week where we sat in
the front pew. I went to a Catholic girl's school until I was 16.

Sex was never talked about when I was growing up. However, my mother
had a huge leather medical dictionary—very large and heavy. She kept it
locked in a bedside table, but that was okay because I knew where the key
was. I was absolutely fascinated by the human body, all the pictures I could
see in that book.

We never talked about sex, except about not getting pregnant. If you did
get pregnant, you were sent in secret to Australia to have the baby and then
have it adopted.

We knew the good girls from the bad girls by how they dressed and what
they did. My dad would test us three girls. He would drive past us as we
walked to or from school, and whistle at us from behind. If any of us turned
around and looked or responded, we were in very deep shit.

And there were other very obtuse signals. We weren't allowed to flirt, basically to even talk to boys. There were three boys who lived next door but we
weren't allowed to mix with them, supposedly because they weren't Catholic.

Until I was twelve, I went to school in town. I didn't have any breasts then
so there was no talk about me. Then I went to a boarding school with sixty
other girls from all over the world. It was Catholic, of course, run by Irish
nuns. There were four hundred day school girls but we didn't mix with them.

We didn't really talk about sex, even in the dormitories, but occasionally we'd hear stories from the day girls. We had an incredible amount of freedom by the time we were fifteen and sixteen years old.

\*\*\*

My dad sexually abused me. Then he started in on my younger sister. He was also an alcoholic, beat up my mother and womanized all over town. Being away from him for four whole years was wonderful to me—I could laugh a lot and I had the whole school grounds to myself much of the time.

Some of us experimented sexually with each other ... well, I did at least. My first lover was a girl two years older than me. It all developed innocently—chatting in the evenings, goodnight hugs and kisses—we lived in the same dorm. It was never more than from the neck up.

Then the Mother Superior heard about it and immediately moved my friend to a different dorm and forbade her from even talking to me. I was young and didn't really understand what was going on but got the clear message that what we were doing was absolutely not okay.

I was sad to lose my friend. She ignored me from then until she graduated. The Mother Superior must have read her the wrath of God.

\*\*\*

Part of being a good girl was that good girls didn't talk about those things. Years later when I got engaged, I found a book—very scientific—combining the psychological and physiological elements of sex. I always wanted to be a dietitian because I really liked learning about the body.

My fiancé saw me with the book and said he was concerned about how much sexual experiences I'd had because I had that book. I couldn't believe it! He assumed I was sexually experienced and not a virgin just because I wanted to read a book about sex!

\*\*\*

I started university at sixteen years old—the British system—where I met a pre-med student. We did a lot of exploring sexually but there was no penetration—I was too afraid of getting pregnant. We were together for about a year. Finally he broke it off because, he said, I was Catholic and he was Jewish so there was no future for us. I was taken aback when I thought about it—I guess I really knew I would marry a Catholic man.

Towards the end of my second year at university I was really struggling. Finally I quit school and went home for six months while I worked as a pharmacist's assistant. I was friends with my dad during this time. We did a lot together, kept secrets from my mother. He took up aerobatics and I'd go along as his passenger/co-pilot. I'd totally blocked out the abuse from my father.

I was still a virgin then, I thought. It weighed heavy on me—I'd allow heavy necking, that was okay, but wouldn't ever let it get out of control. I was really afraid of getting pregnant.

At eighteen, I was still embarrassed about sex. I had very large breasts from an early age and the fellas always looked ... they made no bones about the size of my boobs. If I ever wanted to be myself—you know, playful, funny—the fellas always took it the wrong way. They would come on in a forceful manner and wouldn't take no for an answer. I thought I needed to keep who I was under wraps.

Well into my late 30s, I got the same thing from guys about my boobs and I continued having trouble handling it. I still sometimes play up appearances—cleavage etc., although my breasts got smaller after the children were born—but now it's just for the fun of it.

*****

At nineteen, I wasn't a virgin anymore. I had an affair that year with a man—the affair had a high *no-no* aspect to it. He was married and a person I worked with. He was a thrilling sex partner for me. He knew how to do foreplay for one thing! In retrospect, he was an excellent lover.

I'd been masturbating during my teen years ... but nobody *ever* talked about such things. And, I only did it at home when my mom was out of the house. I'd come home from boarding school and get her book out when no one else was there. Then I would take off my clothes, find her beautiful scarves and dance around her bedroom, building up visual images until I was ready to masturbate. My sexual feelings were very strong.

I still wake up to a climax occasionally, even though it's hard for me to climax with a partner. Even as a youngster, my whole body was a boy-antenna.

When I got engaged, at twenty-two, I put on an act about being a virgin who wouldn't consider masturbating. Still, I was incensed I couldn't have a conversation about bodies and sex without him making me into a bad person for it.

*****

A bad girl was defined as somebody who encouraged boys. I did not do that. I had only coy interaction with boys, no playing. All around me people assumed that if a girl once got one-on-one with a boy, suddenly and automatically she became a bad girl. They didn't even have to do anything.

At university I lived in a Catholic hostel run by Dominican nuns. They were so much fun compared to the Irish nuns in high school! Sure we had restrictions, curfews and things, but I had a private room then. Still, good Catholic girls didn't masturbate and there was no girl/girl sexual action or attractions that I knew about.

Underneath though, I didn't think I was a good girl. Underneath I had deep feelings about my body and sex. I couldn't talk to my mother or my sisters or even my girlfriends. We talked about boy stuff but not about sexual feelings.

The affair I had at nineteen? That made me a very bad girl. It was so exciting to me because I never *imagined* sexual relations could be like that! I was working in the beauty salon part of a big department store. We had one treatment room where he and I would hide and have sex. The anticipation made me crazy. I thought, of course, that I was looking so cool through it all. Ha!

He was a little taken aback that I was a virgin, a good Catholic girl. I had strong feelings about doing it and knowing I wasn't a good girl anymore. I went to confession a lot because I felt so guilty. The priest was always very gentle but when I got the same priest again and again, my penance picked up! He told me I couldn't be seeing this person again but, short of leaving town, I couldn't avoid him.

It worked out. The store sent me 400 miles away to be in charge of another salon at another branch in Auckland. Neither one of us wanted to repeat it when I returned six months later.

While I was away in Auckland, I met someone else. He was Jewish—what was I thinking? He was really sweet and loved me. He wanted us to get married but his parents said no.

Then I met another man who was infatuated with me, another non-Catholic. We got engaged, then I realized he was a total alcoholic—which I wasn't having any part of—so I broke it off.

While I was in Auckland working at the salon, I had several men ... one at a time. There was the boat captain who was very sweet. He treated me very nicely, an older man. He obviously had feelings for me. He would be gone for two to three weeks at a time, so every time we were together was like a reunion. We indulged in very heavy necking although there was no penetration.

Then I met John through my aunt and uncle in Wellington. He was the youngest of seven kids from a very good Catholic family—friends of theirs. He was 27 years old so my aunt and uncle decided he needed to marry a good Catholic girl ... me.

*** 

In my marriage, sex wasn't very good. John was not experienced. If I made any suggestions about how to touch me or how to do things, he got very offended. How did I know that? Even about myself, how did I know that? And I couldn't say that I'd learned that as I masturbated.

We had lots of real problems. The sex just wasn't good. He experienced premature ejaculation the whole nine years we were married. It was nothing like the patience and skill of the man I'd had that affair with, my first real lover.

Unfortunately, I knew what it could be like and that made the marriage even harder. We never talked about sex outside the bedroom and inside the bedroom he'd fall asleep if I tried. I never had an orgasm with him, so I kept on masturbating. We divorced when I was thirty-two.

I moved to Huntington Beach in California. It was the first time I had girlfriends who would talk about sex. It was so much fun to me. I began dating and became serially monogamous ... one at a time because I still had a whole lot of the good girl/bad girl influence. We just pleasured each other, we didn't need to penetrate.

For the first time in my life, I allowed myself pleasure. The whole world opened up, I could be myself. I had the two kids, night school, worked 9-5—I was having a ball! I didn't need a man or masturbation to feel pleasured—just doing what I was doing was a huge pleasure.

***

I never have made sexual pleasure into a big thing in my life. Climaxing with a partner is somewhat problematic for me ... it takes a lot of time. I felt a huge freedom getting out of that marriage—it was a real epiphany for me.

I liked having that series of relationships—I could be me and have fun. One time, for instance ... well, I'm a long time prankster. I can carry a prank on for weeks and months. When I was a commodities broker, I had fun with my buddies shortly before I left. I was studying in personal growth, training to be a trainer, and during that time I met someone very briefly—oh, did I fall for him. There was a real spark. So I wrote him a note, unsigned, about us getting together. I made myself sound real mysterious. This carried on for three or four weeks. I had nothing to lose. I kept sending him notes, he kept sending me back notes.

In the event, we connected in a parking lot. When he realized who I was, he was clearly open to a sexual encounter. We had the most wonderful time at my house for about three hours. It was sweet, fun. The preamble had really been a kick.

I learned it was okay to be who I am, without assuming that a man had to enter me for me to be right. To me, penetration means I'm being raped. I'm not ready for penetration for a very long time after a man is ready. My whole sex life, from the time my father sexually abused me, through my husband and almost all men since then, have felt like rape. Almost no men have a clear motive to have me ready for intercourse, taking the time with me. Most men just aren't willing. Except for my first lover.

I did have a series of brief relationships but they were more of the same. We'd have a lot of verbal foreplay, flirting, kindnesses, but when it came to sex, the patience just wasn't there. The situations that come to mind—they weren't interested in knowing what works for me and what doesn't.

Finally I got to the point of why bother? My sex life has been very uninteresting for the last twenty years. At the same time, I consider myself a sexual, sensual person, just without the sex part.

I've been using a healing instrument for the last eight or nine years. As part of that work, it became clear it's all about relationship for me. As we interpreted different issues in the healing work—like personality, work, sex—it became clear that I'm a 'non-active sexual' person.

Sex has never been a high priority for me. I play with men around sex in order to get their attention! But, when I'm open and flirting, men interpret that in a sexual manner. As I've gotten older, I've learned to stop before we get there. Actually, I've become so disillusioned by the whole thing ...

***

I don't have sexual fantasies. I have a hard time when men go into their fantasies, I want to scream ... 'I'm right here!' Why would men go into that? And, what a waste of time fantasy is. When I self-pleasure, it's not fantasy-based either. It's all about arranging my body to make pleasure happen.

My hottest experience was with a man I worked with. I was a single mother and he participated with me as a member of the family for about a year. He was the only relationship in my life where I felt like I was an important part of the equation in that relationship. He focused totally on pleasing me—his pleasure was in pleasing me. That relationship was worth every moment.

Remember, I'd been a good Catholic girl in a very restricting marriage. For the first time I could do and be who I wanted to be. As I dated, I learned that men are only interested in getting their rocks off. I wanted each new man to be different but he wasn't. I don't think, except for that one exception, that I've ever had a mutually beneficial relationship with a man.

Later, in my forties, I did the work on processing the sexual abuse from my father. Then I began dating a man, an engineer, who was very attractive. We had a lot of playfulness together but eventually I went off to do some other things in my life. I ran into him several years later. We were still attracted to each other so we went out a few times, had a few drinks. We graduated to dinner out, and finally I spent the night on his boat with him.

I decided to tell him about the sexual abuse I've experienced. It was like a giant door closed. He totally shut down and I never heard from him again. That's happened other times too. It would seem some men are just very threatened by it. I've heard other women say the same thing. I would love to have a conversation with other women who've experienced this—how have they handled it?

One man I really liked, well, we played a lot but he wasn't willing to be monogamous and I wasn't willing to not be. He was a good friend, though. So really, I've never had a man to play with where I could also have nice sex— I've never had those together. It would have been very nice for me.

***

What I like most about sex is the lead up, the foreplay. I like sitting at dinner, having a conversation, setting an atmosphere. I like being sexually charged without necessarily acting on it. I guess what I really like is being sensual.

What I like least about sex is penetration. I don't like being forced. I don't like that there's always time for him to get his rocks off, but not time for me to be ready. I want to scream at them ... but I haven't in the past, I've just shut down.

There are several sexual things I won't do. I had one lover who spanked me once. I told him I didn't like it and he stopped. But the next time we made love, he tried it again. When I got upset, he started in on how he thought I'd like it if I'd just let him continue. NO.

I don't like being sodomized. I don't like anything to do with sado-masochism.

When it comes down to it, what I've found most endearing in a lover is when he shows tenderness towards me, not just sexual neediness. Tenderness includes listening to what I think needs to be done to get me going ... and his willingness to help.

I find a man who is empathetic and compassionate to be an endearing lover. Physically, tenderness and foreplay go together ... especially around what I might like in the lovemaking.

I find premature insertion to be most annoying ... especially around vaginal dryness—for God's sake, pay attention!

I will no longer do oral sex. I feel like I'm being throttled. That probably is a throw back from the sexual abuse as a child. My sister has been so scarred by it that she can't bear to even have a dentist's hands in her mouth. And there's the issue of STDs too, like the lover who didn't bother to tell me he had herpes until he had an outbreak! Herpes is a transmittable disease whether it's active or not!

Body odor can sometimes be really annoying too. I like the natural smell of a man, but not following heavy labor or sweating. It's nice when a man showers right before making love, but if it's not rank, his natural body odor is nice too.

There haven't been any major differences pre- and post-menopause. My libido is less but I still feel sensual ... I just don't actually need sex. I've always been that way so it's just gotten a little more so. I'm in my mid-60s and I just recently decided I need some hormones because I'm experiencing some vaginal dryness for the first time.

\*\*\*

I wish I was twenty years old and knew then what I know now. I would want to raise girls instead of boys. I didn't trust women when I was younger, perhaps because my mother never protected me from my father.

But I would raise those girls in real non-traditional ways—educate them at a Montessori or Waldorf school where their spirit and creative expression could blossom and they are allowed to be who they are, not found wrong for being girls.

I wouldn't allow any talk about good girl/bad girl elements. I would be much more understanding and honor their young spirits. The good girl/bad girl paradigm is just so wrong—it doesn't serve us or our community as a whole. I would drop the whole concept!

Being honest, though, I still slip into it when I see young girls walking down the street dressed like ... well, whatever they're dressed like. I worked at a women's hotline/help center for awhile that had big posters up on the wall with photos of young women looking provocative. The caption said—"This doesn't allow you to touch me." I remind myself of that whenever I slip into judging a woman by what she is wearing. I do think that in looking provocative, women draw to themselves men who think it's an invitation. It's not—but it may be where abuse and anger starts for men.

\*\*\*

Yes, I am one of the crones now. When I think about sending a message to the daughters and granddaughters growing up today, I picture an environment—out of Aldous Huxley's book *The Island*—where it is perfectly okay to be sexual and free in your expression. Sexuality is a part of life. Nothing is taboo. You can touch another or yourself—nothing is wrong. That idyllic picture is the message I'd like to send to them.

I would also let them know that that doesn't exist ... yet ... so they have to be responsible for their own bodies. I believe that how a relationship goes is about how she calls the shots. She has to feel able to walk away if her needs aren't being met. And then be willing to walk away.

I think it takes good basic parenting for a young girl, say 12-14 years old, to not be embarrassed by her body. I am so impressed by the Mankind

Project—that movement for men that includes rites of passage and life-changing ceremonies. We really need to do that for women too.

The biggest point I'd make is that it's your body—you get to decide what happens with it. If you're treating your body well, you will attract in good treatment—the velcro effect.

The huge issue, though, is to give up victimization as a woman. Fight the media and religions who promote being a victim, because in truth, how a relationship goes is how a woman allows it to go. I was in my forties before I got clear that men know how women control relationships, even though most men still try to behave in patriarchal ways.

# 8

# Magdalene

**W**hen I think about good girls and bad girls, what comes to my mind is when you're young and just starting to come of age, you hear rumors and you get to know what's good and bad. If you have a mother like I did, the message is not so much spelled out for you as it's clear what's appropriate and what's not appropriate behaviors by what she does.

My mom didn't need to talk about good and bad girls. The way my mother was, she just ... I don't know what she did. She still does it at 87. Whatever power she had over me, she's still got. Somehow you just knew how to behave—raised in a Catholic home, you pick it up here and there.

I didn't know what sex was until third grade when somebody called somebody else a 'fuck' and I said 'Ohhhhh, he called him a fuck. What's a fuck?' The little boy next to me said 'That's when boys and girls rub their peepees together.' The thought of it was just so disgusting to me.

So of course, while I don't remember a time or place in school when the nuns and priests said anything specific, you knew sex wasn't part of the plan. Somehow you picked that up. If that was the response—a kid got slapped across the face and humiliated in front of the whole class because he said the word fuck—you learned that fucking is not a good thing right up front.

What they should have taught us is that fuck is a crude word and you shouldn't say it. It would probably have been sufficient.

***

So I started out with the negative connotation of whatever I imagined sex to be. My experience was that when I was ten years old, a girlfriend of mine said some older boys were going to come by. They were sixteen and I was ten. My friend came from a huge Catholic family and her parents were never around. Her mother had two little babies and they had a maid—the whole rich thing—but I never saw the parents.

I'd go over there and it was just a wild house, all the kids were every place and nobody watching and I loved to go over there because my house was just a little tiny house compared to their big giant one. They had locks on all the refrigerators and all the booze cabinets and the food. With thirteen kids you gotta lock it up because the kids come home with all their friends and they eat everything. The kids were fed three times a day by the maid.

So I get over there and my friend says some boys are coming over. I asked what they wanted. She says they want to fuck. My heart went into my stomach. I had fear and loathing because I didn't want to fuck. But she was going with them because she was really cool ... I thought ... so I went with her.

We went down the street to the guys' fort, which they had dug into the ground. They had lights and everything—it could have been an old crawl hole or something like that. We crawled down into this little room and saw a second little room. My friend went into one room with one boy and the other boy told me to go into the other little dirt room and then he said 'Take your pants down.'

I remember shaking and being totally traumatized. I didn't want to do it but my girlfriend was already in with a boy and everybody else was laughing and seemed to be having a great time. They were boys from the neighborhood—kids I'd seen around—but old enough to know better, maybe fifteen or sixteen years old. And they probably didn't know what they were doing.

Just now I'm realizing they really didn't know what they were doing because when I pulled my pants down to about my knees, he just tried to stick that thing in me as hard as he could and he pushed and pushed and pushed until finally I started to get raw on my skin and my legs and my pubic bone was sore. And finally he didn't do anything, come or get off or anything.

I got out of there. I went home. I was so traumatized over that, until I was much older. For many years I thought I was the bad girl. I did that. And I couldn't go to the church and confess it to the priest. There's no way. It was my secret because I had a choice about going and I had chosen to go with them. It was the wrong choice to make. Eventually I put it out of my mind and didn't think about it ... even though it was always there.

It wasn't until I was much older and I saw my own daughter approaching that age, I saw how young and beautiful and innocent she was. I finally forgave myself. I said wait a minute. Come on, you were only ten years old and they were fifteen. And they probably look back and go, wow. They might have children of their own and look at what they'd done—what did I do to that girl? Or they grew up to be total perverts. Actually one of them is a businessman in town. I could probably find both of them if I really wanted to.

It shaped my overall feeling about my sexuality. By the time I was sixteen, I hadn't had real sex yet but I was a young woman. I had friends. It didn't totally screw my life up. I came from a good family.

But I had problems after it happened. My grades dropped and nobody knew what was wrong with me. I knew what was wrong with me, sort of … mostly in looking backwards—oh, that's why I got a D in history that year. I wouldn't go to school. Or, I would get to school and then I had a stomach ache. I missed three weeks straight in one quarter. There was so much I missed they wouldn't give me a report card and they wouldn't give me grades. It wasn't normal for me. I usually got strong Bs and a few As and Cs. The experience spiraled me down—my self-esteem dropped. I was a sinner and couldn't confess my sins.

By the time I was older I was pretty enough and talented enough and basically smart enough that I hardly had to study and I'd still get a decent grade. With little effort I could still pass school. And I had a lot of friends, I was always happy go lucky and joking around so I just dealt with it.

***

When I was sixteen, I met a boy who became a boyfriend and I married him when I was twenty, stayed with him until I was twenty-five. That was the real beginning of my sexuality..

I started having sex with him when I was sixteen. I probably thought I liked sex—I was as horny as the next girl. Was there guilt about my body? If you want to talk about guilt, that's another story.

Guilt started when I first had sex with him—I got a bladder infection right off. I didn't know what the hell was wrong with me, I thought I was pregnant. Nothing could feel that bad with that much pressure … unless I was pregnant. So I flipped out.

I was only sixteen years old and I was going to a Catholic girl's school in a lilywhite town where everybody knows everybody. My parents were gone on a trip for two or three days and I had such discomfort—my pee was turning orange. I finally took myself to our family doctor. He took a urine sample, told me I had a urinary tract infection and gave me some medicine.

One day before I'd gone to the doctor I called the school and told them I was sick. Then I went down to the beach and just cried my eyes out. One guy came up to me asking, 'What's wrong?' I think I'm pregnant. I told him. Then I laid out my whole sad story.

But I wasn't pregnant—and that's when the whole guilt thing started full force. I'd gotten a reprieve—I was being warned—I had a chance to not do this—I should not do this anymore—it's a sin.

So I had to tell my boyfriend we shouldn't have sex. He said 'I don't think so'—now that he'd had it, he really wanted it. I wasn't very good at turning over my new leaf. I still had sex but I would hold off for a week. It was always this holding off. You wanted to do it but you couldn't do it. You wanted it, you held off. Then we found out about these things called rubbers. And birth control. That was another thing I wasn't supposed to do. So I didn't until I got to college.

Once I got into college it was all different. My best girlfriend got pregnant for me. She's still my best girlfriend after fifty years. She missed the last semester of high school. She had it much harder than I would have. My parents were loving and understanding and her parents were not. I lived through her pain and anguish and watched her give up the baby. I would not have been that brave. I would probably have had an abortion. Back then they had just become legal. You could get some help. You knew it was an option.

\*\*\*

We dated from ages 16-20. And I wasn't always the most faithful person. Nor was he for those first years. I didn't sleep around with a lot of people but we went to different colleges at first and I had another boyfriend and I'm sure he dated another girl. It was normal behavior as I see it now…but back then we tried to keep it secret from each other, of course, because even though we were separated since we were at different schools, we were still closely connected and dating. I do remember, now, though— I slept with one of his fraternity brothers. Not a highlight of my moral history.

Then we married at twenty. There was not a lot of guilt after that. Within the marriage, sex was fun. He is dying of cancer right now. Life goes on and all of a sudden the sex doesn't seem so important anymore. We were so young then, and now I am old…well, older. Time has a way of changing your priorities.

One day, after six months of marriage, he walked in and said he didn't know if he wanted to be married anymore. I couldn't believe it. We'd just had a great big church wedding and now he didn't want to be married!

So we split up for a month. I went to Hawaii to stay with his best friend in a house on the beach in Oahu. I didn't sleep with him. I probably would have—but he wouldn't entertain the thought. I was that bad to even think about it. My husband ended up coming over to Hawaii about three weeks into my trip –to woo me back. I don't think he liked the idea of me loose on the island of Oahu. We finished out our first year of marriage and decided to move away to finish our college educations.

\*\*\*

We were back in college for a hot six months when he walked in again and said, 'I'm moving out and going to live with my buddies.' My parents were going to Cape Canaveral, Florida for my dad's job, so I went with them. It was the unmanned Viking Mission to Mars. My father was involved in that project and it was quite a big deal on the international level.

There was going to be a big party at this beautiful home overlooking the harbor boats and the whole thing. All these important people were going and my dad said 'You have to go with an escort. I don't want you going to this party alone.' I was twenty-two years old. I was black as a berry, had long blond hair, a crop top thing with my belly hanging out. I was hot to trot. And my dad says 'You're going with an escort and I've got him picked out for you.' Well, okay.

When the doorbell rang, it was a man who is fifty years old, a short little Greek guy who is very unattractive. He smoked. He looked like my father and not even as good an image as my father. And he had flowers. He was smart, he was wealthy, he was interesting, he was funny and he adored me. He treated me like a total queen. We didn't get home until four in the morning. We had taken a long walk out on the beach. We talked and talked and talked.

I stayed there for a month and he courted me the whole time. By the end of the month he wanted to marry me but he was old and I didn't want to look at his body anymore. But he was great in bed. He told me he was forty-five, but he was really fifty. I should have married him but I was still married to my first husband.

So I went back home and told my husband this other guy wanted to marry me. And my husband got all jealous and moved back in. We got back together for another couple of years until we graduated. Then we moved back to LA and one day he just didn't come home. Oh, man. Then when he got home, I was gone. So that was the end of that.

There was a period of time between my first and second husbands when I had a boyfriend I lived with, but I dated a lot of other guys too. I was the queen of the town. It was fun. Sorta...

I was searching. I knew what I wanted. I didn't like my job. I didn't like to work. I wanted some man to come and take me away so I could have a baby and have a 'normal' life—which in my mind was staying home with the babies. I thought that was exactly what I wanted.

I ended up with a good man, a very good man. He was a good father and provider. And then that went away. I think I regret it until I spend five minutes with him again ... then I remember—'Oh yeah, that's why I left you. You're really annoying ... but a good person.'

*\*\*\**

Things have changed since then. I don't have the sexual drive that I used to have. When I was in my thirties, my second husband seemed boring and not spontaneous. He irritated me about little things every day so I didn't feel like I wanted to have sex with him.

Even in the beginning … we're laying in bed after the second time we'd had sex and I said, 'Touch me I'm your whore.'

He stopped, aghast, and says, 'Don't talk like that, I can't think of you like that!' And I thought, 'Oh god now I get it. Midwestern, Ohio, German … all right.' I remember laying there thinking 'Okay, this is my trade off. I'm not going to say 'fuck me I'm your whore' because it doesn't fit into his picture of what is appropriate.' After that sex was okay but kinda blah. I chose it though, I remembered that.

When I was forty-two, I started thinking about stuff. Is this how I want to live the rest of my life or do I want to have a real passionate relationship with somebody? So I did.

That was the year I met Mike. I was at peace when I was forty-four, so I must have met Mike when I was forty-two.

When I look back at it, I wasn't satisfied with myself and although my husband wasn't perfect, he wasn't that bad—all things considered he was a pretty damn good husband and father. He was great, actually, just not dynamite in bed, which for me by the time I got to be in my early forties, was enough to make me look elsewhere. But truthfully, for me, I was unsatis-fied—number one with my own personal accomplishments.

I was raising my beautiful daughter but I also felt that was something I was doing for her. One of the things I'm so grateful about from her dad was that I didn't have to work. I spent every moment of my motherhood—her early childhood—home with her, when I wanted to be there. That is something I'll always love and respect him for—giving me that opportunity. Still, what was I doing for me? … not that I didn't get anything out of being a mother.

As a result, parts of me that I could have developed didn't get developed. And I had no one really to blame but myself. I mean, if you want to develop something, godamit, get off your ass and go develop it. The thing was, I didn't realize I probably could have done that and kept my marriage intact. For me, I had to change everything—not just in terms of going from motherhood to going to UCLA medical school, but I had to get divorced on top of it.

Why didn't I just pick one thing and do that, and see how that would change my whole life? Instead I made him the problem and at the same time recognized enough to know I had to do something for myself. So I did both.

If I had only started medical school when I was a little bit younger, I would have had a different relationship with my husband. Part of the problem was me not working and he never pushing me to work. So the longer I was out of the workforce, the less I felt I was capable of going back into it. I felt trapped.

I had an epiphany at some point, thinking to myself. 'Wait a minute, Magdalene. You're going to be lying on your death bed, taking your last breath, wondering 'Is this my last breath, is that my last breath?' Are you gonna say to yourself, wait a minute, I didn't even try. I didn't even try to do something? I just let life go by me? Roll on because it was easy? Because my husband was taking care of me and I didn't have to do anything but go shopping and go hiking, take the dog to the vet, pick up my daughter?' And I didn't even try to push myself, to do something a little bit more than that?

I said to myself, 'You know what, even if I fail I'm gonna go give it a shot.' When I finally accepted that I could fail at something, that's when I was able to go and accomplish something. So I did it all. Divorced, went to school.

\*\*\*

The sex was great with my new boyfriend. Oh my god. And my poor husband was devastated. But I couldn't do both of them—I'm not that kind of person. By the time I was with Mike I was finished with Wayne. I knew it was over even if he didn't know it yet. He eventually figured it out. Age old story. Now I've been with the same man ... well, it's been fourteen years.

What changed for me when Mike came into my life was that I got great sex. Of course, there was more to our relationship than that—but the difference was so profound in that area. I felt I could love with abandon, in any way ... and not be judged for it ... not be made to feel like I was the bad girl but that I was the good girl. So, that is more what it was like. As time goes by, the sex still changes and grows.

Still, people change. In the beginning it was new and fresh—wonderful. It's not any different than when you're young. Time goes by, then it's 'did you take out the fucking trash?' We women just swap one in or another one out. In many ways, they're all the same, in the end. I'm just teasing...

It's not all about sex, either. That was my excuse to get away from Wayne—it's an easy segue. 'Oh, great sex, I'll just go in that direction.' Mike was so generous and all these things that my husband wasn't. Wayne was more tight and controlled and miserly by nature. What can I say—he's frugal.

\*\*\*

I didn't work, then, so whatever money he gave me was like $100 a week ... at first it was $70. And I'm supposed to clothe myself, my daughter, all of us, and feed all of us on $70 a week?

I wasn't privy to what he made and I didn't see him do the bills. He's say, 'Don't worry your pretty little head, I'll just give you your stipend every week.' On the weekend, he would pay for whatever we did, pull out the credit card.

After a while it started bugging me. I'm not a wilting violet, I'm a strong assertive woman. Once I was at my mother's house and I started my period. I went up to my husband and said, 'Do you have $5?' 'Why?' 'Because I need to go to the drugstore.' In front of everybody, he goes, 'Why?'

'Just gimme a fucking $5 so I can go to the drugstore, it's not your business why.' I didn't say that. What I did say was 'I have my period and no one has tampons and I have to go buy myself a box of kotex.' So I humiliated him. I made him look like an asshole, which he was being.

So here's how he takes his money out of the wallet, one bill at a time. He peels off a $5 bill like he just couldn't stand letting go of it. I'll always remember that. Why couldn't he be one of those men who goes, 'Hi honey. What do you need, honey? Here, take my wallet, honey.'

Now I have one of those men. And he's a good-hearted idiot because he doesn't have any responsibility. He's just like I used to be. I figured out, after living with Mike for eight years, just how much of a sweetie he is. Up until then, he'd say, 'Oh you want to go to San Francisco now? Let's go.' And we'd just go. We would go out shopping. He would say, 'Oh you look so cute, here put on this hat and this necklace and a pair of shoes. Oh now you look great.' He loved to take me shopping and buy me things.

And then one day I was looking for something and I went into his walk-in closet where he's got a desk and all his paperwork is there. I saw his gasoline bill. It was $6,000. He was working out of town and had to drive a long distance every day. He charged gas and he would just pay the minimum at the end of the month on the charge card. I found his credit card—$13,000. What the fuck is this?

So I took over and cleared it all up. Now his paycheck comes into my account. I control everything that has to do with money. I became my ex-husband and now I'm the asshole. So I have enough appreciation to realize there really should be more of a blending of two people beyond sex, where the funds come in. Sometimes it requires one person to take care of it, when the other doesn't have a fucking clue. And so now, sometimes I feel like I'm the man.

***

Oh yeah, I orgasm! Mike is pretty conscious. Actually, I'm not particularly interested in oral sex, I don't like it in general. It makes me cringe. I have friends who say, 'Oh I love it, that's how I get off.' Why would you want your face down there? But, all right, they like it.

My second husband was the best with oral sex. For some reason he just knew what to do. Most men think that if they lick everything it feels good. No. no, no, it's a little more specific than that. Anyway, so I just kinda don't care for that part of it. I'm not opposed to it, but usually it's in the beginning of the relationship. As relationships progress, the sex gets more and more confined, always the same.

**\*\*\***

I can orgasm by myself without thinking about anything. I don't have to think about a man, it's a physiological function. 'Okay, that feels really good. Okay. Okay. Okay. Go on to work now.' It doesn't have to be any big deal. I don't think about anything.

When I was younger I'd have a fantasy about walking down this way and Tom Selleck comes around the corner, then Steve McQueen. I can have fifty men around me in my fantasy. But in reality, I don't want to actually live it.

During medical school I learned how to not think about anything when I masturbate. I had to do a rotation at a local organization, where they are very religious, very fundamentalist. So I get my first patient, a black guy. He says to me, 'I got something white coming out of my penis.' Sure enough he's got this white stuff coming out of his penis. I go running into my supervisor, 'This guy's got white stuff coming out of his penis!' He says, 'It's semen.' '*What? Why wouldn't he know what it is?*' I was feeling a little hysterical at that point.

My supervisor told me, 'Oh, well, because of our teaching here, we tell them that if they want to get help from the mission, they have to follow our program. In our program, we don't masturbate. It's a sin. So they don't masturbate. Then they wake up in the morning and they've ejaculated in their sleep and they don't know what's wrong. They think something is coming out of their penis.'

To me, that's sick. 'What kind of a god is it that requires a creature to have orgasms. Then sends you along to sit there and tell them they're not allowed to do that? It's contraintuitive. It doesn't make any sense. What is so bad about masturbating?'

He said, 'It's not the act itself, it's really what you think about when you're doing it.'

'Like, okay, so you're not supposed to think about fucking your neighbor's wife. Okay. What happens if you think about food? Is that a sin?'

Then he said, 'I suppose if you think about food, it's not a sin.'

Well, nobody thinks about food when they are masturbating. And then I thought about thinking about nothing. And I thought about it for awhile and now I can have an orgasm without thinking about sex or any person or food. You don't have to have some big fantasy thing going, it's just a physiological thing. So what I say about masturbation being a sin is—what a bunch of bullshit!

***

Well, I mean, an orgasm is an orgasm. I usually have three. The first one takes me awhile. The second and third come right on top of each other.

I am blessed because I have a partner who also has multiple orgasms, so he can go and go and go. I know that isn't the case for many men, especially his age. He's phenomenal somehow. He's just really good ... like the best. He's this little guy, a pain in the ass, a temper on him, but damn is he good in bed. He just is. Even though we're not all that wild anymore, he knows exactly how to get me.

When I watch people on porn flicks—upside down and all these positions, I can't do that. I have to have a certain position and I have to hold my arms a certain way and I have to squeeze in a certain spot. And then I have to ask myself 'can I have one, am I going to have one? I think it's coming ... it's coming. Oh yeah, oh yeah.' And then I have it and then relax enough to be able to have another one. But that first one is the hardest one. I always wonder how other women are that way.

I suppose I'm not nearly as repressed as I think I am. Actually, I just am what I am ... but ... I sometimes think that really I could do without sex altogether. Sometimes I think it's got to do with my first contact with those boys when I was ten. It was such a horrible thing that happened to me that it jaded me and made me different. Then I get the urge and I change my mind. The reality is that part of me doesn't like it, doesn't want it. Wants it but doesn't want it.

I think I always buried my first sexual encounter—the one when I was ten—somewhere inside me and it caused me to always feel on some level that I could do without sex, but then the reality of hormones and desire came into play and it felt so good, I would be overcome and I wanted it just as much as anyone could want it.

I am sure it's got to do with my first contact with those boys. It was such a life altering thing that happened to me that it jaded me and made me different. Through the years I've dealt with it, and I understand intellectually but there's other stuff going on that I may never figure out ... nor do I care to, at this point in time. It's not like I had a totally abnormal sex life. I think I had a pretty normal sex life.

I don't think I'm highly sexed, I don't think I'm undersexed. If I average out across my whole life, I'd be average, whatever that is. I wanted sex a lot when I was younger. I liked the newness of sex, with a new person, I liked that beginning part. I loved that when I was younger.

Back when I was single, I had, maybe, two one night stands and suddenly it seemed kind of creepy. I made the mistake of meeting somebody and going home with him and all of a sudden I'm in the middle of sex and realizing I don't really want to do this. But I'm in the middle of it and he's just going on. I'm laying there going, 'I don't think so.' That's when I grew up. 'I don't need to do this, I can have sex with anybody. I just need to find the right person to do it with.' You learn that pretty young if you're lucky. Just one or two of those experiences and you go, 'Nahhh, don't need to do this anymore.'

It's interesting because now I work with kids who were sexually molested. And they have all kinds of really sick inappropriate behavior. When I compare my experience to the lives of some of the kids I work with, I feel very lucky. I feel like my trauma was more like kids just being kids. I wasn't traumatically raped. I was just put in a situation where I was highly embarrassed. He didn't really do anything to me. He didn't really scare me. He was just pushing against me. I was more afraid of going to hell than being physically injured. I still don't like to be in close places, though. Don't put me in a small room. Sometimes I think it's from that experience.

***

What I like about sex is the intimacy of it, the connection. I like when you really do have sex and look in that person's eyes and you really do tell him you love him and you really mean it. There's nothing like that, to have that with somebody.

The problem is, usually, as time goes by and I get older, the sex occurs less often. The excitement of any relationship tapers off over time. The driving force and sheer intense desire has diminished. But that does not mean that when I am in the moment it isn't intense. My orgasms are more powerful now, even if I have to work harder to achieve them. And I am not nearly as inhibited as I used to be, although, hell, I still struggle with that Catholic bad girl guilt on some level, I am certain.

The only thing I can think of that I don't like about sex is the ickiness factor. My vagina's got fluids down there. I don't want to smell it or touch it or feel it. I never could understand why guys would want to go down there. It's disgusting. So I have this misogynistic approach to my own body. It's impure, it's not good. It's unhealthy to go down there. By the same token, I don't really mind going down on a guy. At least theirs is outside their body and you can see that it's just normal skin you're sucking on.

Before I was in medical school, when I was in my thirties, I realized I never had seen the inside of a vagina. So, I took a mirror and I tried to look up my vagina at my mucous membranes. I'd never done it in my life. It never occurred to me to look at it. Then, when I started medical school, I had loads of patients and I had to look at vaginas all day long. They are not quite so disgusting anymore. I have more of a clinical view.

It's just skin, another kind of skin. I'm not quite as disgusted any longer, but there's still something . . . well, for instance, say I just came home from working out. 'Why do you want to have sex now? Let me take a shower first!'

***

To me, endearing always means a sense of humor. If you can't have a sense of humor in bed, you won't have any fun. Goofing around is fun. It's laughter. I remember Mike and I—especially when we first got together—we'd be having sex and a full on conversation, talking about something that had nothing to do with sex, something else. And enjoying the hell out of it! What'd you think about the movie last night? Or, what shall we have for dinner tomorrow night? We would have a conversation about anything. You gotta laugh and be able to laugh at yourself. It's no fun otherwise. Don't take things too seriously. It's not that big of a deal.

What I find most annoying is when you tell a partner that you like or don't like something in bed and they don't listen to you. I don't like that. Quit doing that. I don't say it like that but they keep doing it however I say it. You say things like, 'Don't start so fast. Take it a little bit slower. I'm older now, I might rip. Slow down. Wait a minute. Give me a chance. Hold on to your horses. You're acting like we're totally into it when we've just begun. I need more time!' But do they listen? Well, I figure if they care enough, they do.

I'm lucky because I have somebody who's willing to take the time. I've talked to other friends who are not so lucky, who complain all the time about their husbands. The guys give up the ghost too easily.

For the guys over fifty, the staying power goes away. Or they have no desire. I've noticed with Mike that the desire is not what it used to be. And of course you can take that personally, I probably have to some degree, at times. He's fifty-nine—why should I expect him to be forty-five when he's not? By the same token, sometimes I'm relieved because I'm not forty-five anymore either. I don't need to have sex all that often, not like we used to anyway.

Often is a subjective term—what does that mean anymore? I think people lie on all of those surveys. They say they have sex more than they really do. I might be wrong. Whenever I hear what the averages are, I always think that sounds like an awful lot. Once a week, maybe, but five times a week? Who are those people? Certainly not me, not even in my youth. Maybe with my first husband but it was only at the very beginning when we stayed up all night long having sex until you can't breathe anymore, until the intensity wore off. After awhile, you get into a routine. When you're younger, it's more frequent.

I just can't imagine people married fifty years and they're doing it all the time. I wonder what the average is for people my age. I have no idea. I have some friends who say they never have sex anymore.

***

I'm fifty-five and done with menopause. I think I have more sex drive since menopause because I was such a prisoner of my hormones, my menstrual period. I remember calling my doctor wondering why I was so angry. Two weeks before my period I would get into a rage over nothing, I wanted to kill, or get pissed at somebody—whoever was in my way. I don't do that anymore, all pissed off and aggravated. Now, I'm so much more even tempered. I don't think it's my living arrangements or because I've changed men. Back then it was like something came over me I couldn't control. Now, without all the hormones raging, I'm more even tempered, more open, more relaxed. That all changed around menopause.

And also I don't expect myself to be perfect—this is what I am. My body image has gotten pretty shitty. I look at pictures when I was young—I was absolutely perfect. Come on, I was an athlete, I was great. And now I'm looking at the rolls on my stomach and my little thing right here.

I shaved it. I wondered why these girls are shaving their pubic hair. They look like little girls, prepubescent. What man would want a prepubescent girl? I started doing pap smears and all the young women were coming in shaved … herringbone, landing strips, the whole design thing. So one day in the shower I shaved it all off. It looked like a little blubbery thing. Better to have hair so I don't see the fat … not to mention the cesarean section scar.

***

My definition of good girl and bad girl is still the same. The bad girls fuck around and do all the bad sex things. And the good girls keep their legs together and wait until marriage. I'm half kidding. Part of me does still feel partly like that.

I have a daughter, and as she grew up, I tried to teach her that she was special enough to be selective. I didn't lay a big guilt trip on her…well, not too much anyway…guilt does work, you know. It makes people not do things they would like to do for fear that something bad will happen to them. It keeps kids in line if they know their parents are waiting in the wings to take them out if they screw up.

I think I was different from my mom, not in most ways, but in one impor-tant way. I spoke up more about sex. I talked to my daughter about sex. But my parents never talked to me about sex. I had an older sister but we didn't talk about sex either. I can't remember talking to anybody about sex. I remember my mom talking to me about periods—that was about it.

But I did talk to my daughter. When my daughter was in kindergarten, I told her I had to fill out a form about her. I needed her name, date of birth and her sex. 'OHHHHH. You said sex!' I realized that she thought sex was a really bad word. I asked her what she thought sex meant. 'I can't tell you, I can't.' she answered. She's five! So I got out a piece of sidewalk chalk. 'You draw me a picture of what you think sex is. You just draw the picture, I won't get mad, I think it's very interesting and because I want to tell you if you're right.'

So she drew a picture of a girl with her legs spread and with a boy's head right there. I go, 'Sort of, but let me draw you a picture of what sex really is. You got the girl right. But now, the boy with arms and legs and there's his penis and it goes into the girl. That's what sex is so if somebody tells you something different, you know what it means.' Now she's twenty-two … she survived.

I was so paranoid the same thing was going to happen to my daughter that happened to me when I was ten. So finally I told her about my experience when she got to be twelve years old. I tried to explain to her how it affected me in my life, in a way that was age appropriate for her. I like to think she didn't … I don't know … get *hurt* in her sexual experiences. Actually I don't know what her experiences have been. She seems well adjusted enough and has had her share of boyfriends. I guess it's not really any of my business. At least not any more than my sex life being my mother's business.

To me, a good girl is somebody who can be honest about herself and be responsible for her actions. And know that her actions don't just affect herself but other people's lives and feelings, and know that all of that comes around back to her.

If your motivation is out of greed and self-centeredness, you're not going to get something positive back. If your motivation is out of openness and caring and love, you'll usually get that back to you. If you don't, then it really has nothing to do with you, it has to do with the other person. So usually you get back what you create—most of the time.

A good girl is one who tries to live by the principle of honesty and openness and love. And being willing to accept what they get in turn and recognize it for what it is. Recognize the part that they are responsible for and the part the other person is responsible for.

A bad girl is one who doesn't do those things, who is only concerned about how she feels, not how the other person feels.

I don't know if there is such a thing as a bad girl sexually. Bad by whose standards—society? To the typical society or religion, a bad girl is somebody who fucks everybody in sight, a prostitute, someone who sells her body, who has no respect for herself. You can say that, but in my experience, where you see people who've been sexually abused as children, their behavior can border on the bizarrely psychopathic.

I have seen children smear themselves in feces and eat it; or a young girl entice the boys at school into the boy's bathroom and give them all blow jobs. Yes, it is extreme behavior, but what was done to them was extreme abuse. The so-called 'bad girl' who slept with all the boys on the football team, was most likely victimized in some way, shape or form.

So was she really responsible for her actions? She didn't do that abuse to herself. Perhaps somebody did that to her—fucked her over literally and figuratively when she was little. Abused girls get mixed signals—they know their father had sex with them and they think that's supposed to be love.

That's not a bad girl. That's an injured child. They grow to adulthood without understanding why they act that way, anymore than when they were ten years old. Who am I to judge if they are bad or good? What does it really mean?

My experience of life tells me something other than good and bad labels. Those people who act in that manner—like the pedophile—what they do to children is abhorrent. But we have to remember … they usually are just perpetuating what was done to them. They can't see it because they're sick and they can't control it. Sex is a primal urge, even sick sex, and it makes people do all kinds of crazy shit. It can motivate people to murder. It is a very powerful force within and it can be used for good or bad purposes.

I'm watching a friend right now who's been married for 30 years—the one who had the baby and gave it away when we were seventeen. After the baby was born, my friend and the baby's father went to college and got engaged, split up, then she got married and he got married but to other people. Well, thirty years later the baby found them and now they've met each other again.

And I'm watching her deconstruct her marriage, because she's come in contact with this man who was her soul mate at the age of seventeen. She's decided that he can give her what she wants, which right now happens to be really great sex. Of course, who am I to judge? Didn't I basically do the same thing? And, he may also provide her with the happiest years of her life…yet to come. So these are interesting questions we're talking about because I've been thinking about this stuff lately, mainly because of her.

I don't like her very much right now. I'm trying not to judge her but I've told her I don't agree with what she's doing, if only because, from my own experience, she's justifying her actions and she's not being responsible and having integrity to the one person that's put up with all her bullshit for the last thirty years—the man who's been her husband.

I see her sex urge is so strong … and she's my age. The energy she's got right now for sex is way out there. My sex drive increased after menopause and I think, well, I just have more now. But that much more? To the point of distraction? I don't get it.

***

I don't know if I'm the person to ask about wisdom. Maybe—definitely—I'm still on my journey. These are questions I haven't thought a lot about from that perspective.

So, perhaps I would say to my daughters and granddaughters—just enjoy it. Enjoy yourself. Get past your body image shit. In general, we women have such a poor body image of ourselves. We look in the mirror and see fat blob. The fat guy looks in a mirror and sees a handsome fit guy. Men have better self-images, woman have lesser self-images.

If we could only teach our young women that their bodies are okay. The important thing is to be healthy and enjoy who you are, rather than what Madison Ave. tells you you're supposed to look like. Those folks are all screwed up. I watch women get their face surgery, tummy tucks and boob jobs—it's weird. Although I wouldn't mind having a face lift. I'd like to have my eyes back. How confused am I?

I really don't have any problems with cosmetic surgery. I always said I was just going to grow old gracefully, until I actually started to grow old. I'd like the whole forehead lift, bringing my eyebrows back up to the bone. I've got two boobs that droop. But at least I have boobs. I have several friends who have had theirs lopped off due to cancer.

The young girls just have to be self possessed and know they're okay the way they are and not feel like they have to have sex. I think that when kids are young, they think they have to do things supposedly everybody else is doing, even when they're not sure and don't really know if they want to.

Be really damn sure that's what you want to do before you do it. We came up in the 60s and 70s, but the 70s was way more promiscuous, paved by the 60s. I lost friends in the 80s because of AIDS. That's a hard reality that you want to teach young kids.

Nancy Reagan's 'Just Say No?' Well, all right. Sometimes you should just say no, sometimes that's okay. I used to see my daughter, wanting to have a boyfriend so bad, at twelve or thirteen. You're so afraid as a parent. You let them out a little more by themselves, as they grow. They walk around town a little more. It was scary to me and all it takes is one time with the wrong person and your daughter is a victim.

But they don't really listen, any more than I did. They're not any different, it's just that the risks are higher now. Back in my day the worst thing we thought we could catch was herpes. Now, give me herpes, just don't give me AIDS.

# 9

# Beth

The whole good girl/bad girl thing was definitely a part of my life, mostly because my mother always talked to me about wanting the 'good girl' to come back. From a very early age, she started saying that to me.

In fact it was a major problem that took me many years to resolve. She used to get angry and yell at me to send the 'bad' me away—she wanted the good me back. She had this good/bad dynamic, that she didn't like half of me to start with. That started from very early, at least four years old but probably earlier. She was very prudish too, so a lot of things got tangled into this good and bad concept for me, including sexuality.

Early on in school there wasn't much talk of good girls and bad girls. I started junior high in California and it wasn't as big a problem. We moved to Texas when I was thirteen. There, the concept was more pronounced and more of a social dynamic. There were the good girls and the bad girls ... period.

Anything sexual was bad. That didn't just relate to sexual activity with a partner. If you dressed sexually, that counted in junior high. Oddly enough, breasts didn't matter very much. I did develop fairly early, but when I was ten or eleven I was still in California. By the time I got to Texas, I was pretty much used to my breasts. About eleven or twelve, I was kind of proud of them. It made people think I was older.

By high school, any kind of sexual activity was a real taboo. You had to worry about your reputation. We all knew who the bad girls were. In fact, at my high school we had two prostitutes and everybody knew it. One of them went on to be first runner up to Miss USA for the Miss Universe pageant. Both of them were very attractive.

I always felt like I was a good girl. One time in high school, I went out with a guy I'd been wanting to go out with for quite a while. He tried to feel my breasts and I got out of the car and left the date. Later, after my parents went to bed, I got dressed and snuck out to go over to my friend's house. I threw rocks at his window, woke him up and then we talked about what had happened.

This is the same guy who kind of turned me around sexually, at about sixteen—he was my best friend. He was a year older than me and went off to the University of Texas. I went to Mexico and then came out to California to stay with my grandmother for awhile. He wrote me letters to tell me that he'd had sex twice and it wasn't anything like I thought it was. It wasn't an end, it was a means to an end.

Later, we ran into each other again after we were adults and we laughed about it. He was so responsible for my sexual life. If he had not written those letters ... when I first got them I thought of it as a betrayal, because we used to talk about everything and I thought it was a betrayal that he'd had sex without me. Later, I thought about his letters differently ... after I had my first sexual experience, when I was a senior in high school. I was sixteen.

***

We talked about sex among girl friends at school. At home, my father talked about sex. My mother would get upset because my father had a kind of club with friends and us kids when he would tell dirty jokes. My friends were just amazed that I would tell dirty jokes. They wanted to know where I'd heard that. I liked saying my dad told me.

My dad and I have always been very open with each other about a lot of things. Anything that I couldn't talk to him about was my problem, my inhibition, not because I couldn't talk to him about it. My mother was the opposite ... except that they would talk to me about their sex lives and it would drive me crazy. Not the details, though. My mother would say my dad was a sex fiend, and my dad would complain that my mother was frigid.

I didn't ever talk to him about my own sexuality because I felt a very strong religious component. My dad's message to me was basically predictable—I needed to worry about my reputation. My parents never talked about love-making being good.

One time I went to a football game. I was with my girlfriend and her family and it started to rain, so we walked home. While it was raining really hard, we went under the bleachers and I made out with her brother. He gave me a hickey. When I got home my parents had an absolute fit. They got the preacher to come talk to me because they assumed I had had sex. It took two or three days before I finally realized why they were so upset and then I was able to tell them that nothing had happened.

My grandfather was a Southern Methodist preacher. My whole family at that point was Lutheran. I had gone through Lutheran confirmation. But I was always the seeker. In my early teens, I decided I needed to find out what I believed, not what my parents believed. By sixteen, I had read the Bible, Koran, Torah and the Book of Mormon. It was around that same time that I quit going to church, which made my mother furious. She grounded me, thinking I would get hit by a car before I got over my religious wandering. My dad finally told her to just leave me alone.

But I had been very active in the church. They had to get permission for me to be the elected secretary of the church because I needed to sign the mortgage papers and legally I was too young. I was *that* active and well known.

***

I married my high school boyfriend when I was eighteen. We lived in different places because he went to Rice University and I went to the University of Texas but we were still together. I came home and spent time with him during the break and I got pregnant. It's probably good I wasn't really promiscuous because I would have been pregnant fourteen times by the time I got out of high school. Birth control never really worked for me.

Sex was great. It was everything my old friend had said it could be in the letters. It made things better in that it made my husband and I closer ... I felt sexy and I felt good about that. At that point I had switched to the University of Houston's chapel as a spiritual center, but my primary involvement was that I played the guitar for the Catholic and Episcopal services—Jefferson Airplane, Simon and Garfunkel ... fun stuff.

We decided to get married when I got pregnant. He stayed in school and I went to work. I did not have that baby but I did have an abortion—I'd had rubella in the first trimester. I was five and a half months pregnant when I had the abortion. It was very difficult for me—I became suicidal. I wanted the baby. I was already very attached to it and it had taken that long for three doctors and my father to talk me into the abortion. It was done in a hospital, reported as a miscarriage ... but it was an abortion.

We were married almost a year. I had a nervous breakdown—which covers a lot of things and actually I'm not sure what it really means.

Texas has weird laws about custody—I was either in the custody of my father or my husband until I was twenty-one, even though my husband wasn't over twenty-one. So my father went to a judge and had custody of me turned back over to him and he had me committed. While I was committed, my father filed for divorce on my behalf and I didn't know whether I really wanted to divorce or not. I had been so suicidal after the abortion and didn't realize it was all hormone fluctuations. I had a tendency to depression anyhow.

I was very confused at the time. When he had me committed, I didn't know I was running a fever, had strep throat and tonsillitis. I was in for thirty days, as long as they could hold me. They got me leveled out. Some of the things they did helped, but the psychiatrist was an idiot. To him everything was my mother's fault and I didn't agree with him about that.

When I got out, I went back to school. I started dating again and I started having sex again … then I got pregnant again. Once I was pregnant, I had to stop school again and this time I decided I wasn't going to get married right away. I wasn't really sure of this guy. He pressed the issue by inviting his family from out of state to our wedding, which I didn't know about at the time. He pushed me into it because he was afraid I would just leave and take his kid with me, which I'm sure would have happened—absolutely. He was right about that.

I was married that time for about seven years. During that period, I had three children. I got pregnant on every form of birth control there is and I even used multiples. I was nineteen when we married, only a little over a year after the first marriage.

He was abusive and when I finally decided I had to get out of there, I kept getting pregnant. He raped me late in the marriage. Early on it was mental and physical abuse. That marriage was very very traumatic and dramatic.

With my first husband, for me to have an orgasm, we didn't even have to be undressed, this guy turned me on so much. With the second husband, sometimes I did, sometimes not. And especially the longer he was abusive, the more I really didn't want to have sex with him. I was hoping he'd have an affair and leave me alone.

I did masturbate and I always orgasmed. I also had affairs later on, while I was still married to him. I was not at all monogamous. The first two years I did stay pregnant and monogamous—my daughters are thirteen months apart. But my son was born two years after the last girl, so I had a little time in there.

I decided I wanted out and that's when I found out I was pregnant with my son. I was hospitalized six times during that pregnancy and found out I had cancer. I couldn't leave during that time, even though I'd already told him I wanted a divorce. I didn't actually get out of there until my son was two.

I think that, at that point, I was using sex to find a man because I really wanted out and away from the abuse. I was afraid of my husband and I felt I needed somebody, like a boyfriend, to back me up, which was a stupid idea but …

My parents hated my second husband, but they wouldn't help me. When I finally did leave, my parents wouldn't help take care of my kids either, no family support there at all—one of the reasons it was so difficult.

Then my ex stalked me—there weren't any stalker laws then. A police officer pulled me into her office—a rare woman in the Houston police department at that time—and she told me to go buy a gun and shoot him. She said 'I've seen this before and if you don't, he's going to kill you.' It was that serious a situation.

I wasn't going to do that, there's no way. I chose to outsmart him. He had been in law school when I left. His school was part of the good old boys legal network in Houston and he was in the thick of it.

A few years before, my father had stood up to some politicians in the area who were involved with the mafia—until they started threatening my brother and me. We found out the divorce judge was very involved in that group.

My father intervened again for me—'I'm going to come get you, you've got to get out of Texas.' All that judge had to do was figure out who I was and I was in trouble.

Between that judge and my ex—being a new lawyer and part of the old boy's club—my divorce decree was a joke. I got all the bills, he got all the assets and the kids. The only reason he took the kids was because he knew he could hurt me that way. I didn't really care about anything else—he could have the stuff, it didn't matter to me.

Eventually I moved to California without the kids and got situated here. Then I went back to Texas and filed for custody under a different judge. It was rough ... but I got my kids back.

\*\*\*

During that time in California, between husbands, I dated but I wasn't sexually active with anybody special. I learned a lot about sex I hadn't known. Basically ... sex became great once I was single. I'd been with two guys at that point and I was very inexperienced, even though I'd been married. So I learned a lot—I was able to be more experimental ... and I wasn't worried about consequences either, because I'd had my tubes tied after my son was born.

I had a lot of fun. There was one guy, we used to call him my YB, Young Buck, because he was about five years younger than me—a body builder and extremely good looking. We were friends—we didn't have a serious relationship and we dated other people. We'd do things like we'd go out on a date and if it was a flop, we'd call each other and then we'd have sex with each other. We were good friends.

Toward the end of the bad marriage, I was reading Erica Jong and my thinking had changed. I didn't feel like there were any taboos at that point. No guilt at all. I decided to try what guys had been doing for years. I was working at Cowboy, which is a bar in Houston—my second job because I had all these bills from the marriage. The uniforms at Cowboy were just like the Dallas Cowboy cheerleaders, pretty skimpy.

There was a drug seller ... who was absolutely gorgeous. I flirted with him until he asked me out. Then I had a one night stand and dumped him because I just wanted to feel what that felt like. That one—I felt guilty about it ... I felt I had behaved badly. He did call me several times after that and all I had intended to do was go out and have sex with him. That was it.

Eventually, here in California, I went to work for a little company in Simi Valley. The way Harry likes to tell it, I left that company for a better position—as his wife.

***

With Harry, everything was different. We were friends before we were ever sexually involved. And we still are. He's still my best friend. I was almost 30 when we met, in 1982. It was actually Harry that financed the custody suit.

Harry and I have been together twenty-six years. When I think in terms of exploring my sexuality, most of it has been done with Harry—reading things, talking about things, discovering things. I don't consider any of it to be separate from sex. Even when I was in the hospital with my gut cut open, he wanted to see into my gut. To me, that connects. He's the only person I really felt comfortable with seeing my open gut. Ha, ha! It could have been weird but with Harry, I knew it was out of love.

Part of the problem we have now is all the chronic pain things that I have. At this point, there's a lot of times when I just really can't have sex, because either I'm in terrible pain or I'm on pain medication and don't feel anything.

Only very occasionally do I orgasm with Harry. Before all the medications I used to. And Harry is a very considerate lover, he's always been very caring about what I like, what I feel—more so than anybody else I've ever encountered. But that also makes sense because he's the person I care about and cares about me the most.

I was in a car accident and we didn't have sex for probably two years—not intercourse anyway. There's a lot of things Harry and I do that I consider to be all in the continuum of the physical relationship between us ... little things like holding hands ... walking by and squeezing my butt ... whatever. It's all part of sex.

I haven't been totally monogamous. There was a guy who was a family friend, back when we still had kids at home. He was having problems in his marriage and he would talk to me, until we ended up developing a relationship. I had sex with him once.

Then there was a situation after Harry started working at his new job, my granddaughter and I were in Mexico and apparently Harry spent the night with one of his students. What's really weird was his reaction to it. He claimed they didn't have sex but the purpose of the whole thing had been his ego. He knew he could have.

Of course I was pissed as hell because he didn't come home that night. Not only was he being unfaithful but he caused a lot of other problems with childcare and people getting to their night job. We had a big blowup about that. But those were the only two times during our marriage we weren't monogamous. He never knew about the time with me.

***

What's changed sexually for me over the years? I started peri-menopause when I was 35. By the time I was 45, I was done. Actually, during menopause, not much changed. There were the two years when I was totally disabled, injured too badly. After that, I gained a lot of weight from the medications. One reason I felt okay about myself, was that no matter how much weight I gained, Harry was still sexually aroused by me. That was a very positive influence on my sexuality, knowing it didn't matter what size I was. Before it was all over, I weighed 346 pounds, during the '90s. Then it came off again.

I went through a short period of time when I was having difficulty even being aroused. It was right around 2000, when I was in my late forties. My doctor decided it had to do with the medications I was taking. He switched me to something with a bit more testosterone which seems to have fixed me up.

My sex drive has stayed about the same since then. The one thing that interfered was PMS ... Harry didn't want to be around me during that time of the month!

***

I like the way sex feels, the intimacy of it, the connection to another human being. But I can also be intimate with myself and that's satisfying too. Intimacy means a close connection that's both emotional and physical. It's not just sexual things, it's touching and little things.

I've never liked oral sex. I feel like I gave it a shot and tried it enough different ways. It really doesn't make that much of a difference if he does me or I do him. It's just not my preference. I don't hate it. I'm able to do it and not be upset about it ... but it's just never been my thing.

I won't do anal sex.

Sometimes I fantasize and sometimes I don't. There's only a little bit of difference in how it feels, even when I self-pleasure. If I fantasize while I'm with Harry, it's actually a fantasy that involves a real human, him or someone else. Occasionally, during masturbation, I'll have a fantasy with a stranger—that's the only difference.

Sometimes I'll have erotic dreams and whatever I wake up with, that's the hottest fantasy at the moment. Whatever and however that scenario worked out in the dream, it was great. It becomes the fantasy of the month or the week or the whatever. It's not always the same and there are things in the dream that come totally from my subconscious. They don't seem to have real themes that run through them.

That old friend I told you about, while I was between husbands? We tried a lot and did a lot sexually, together. He loosened me up … really taught me a lot of new stuff. He taught me to be playful and not to be afraid of trying new things, not to be afraid to trust another human. He taught me all kinds of new sexual techniques. That was pretty hot.

I had never even considered using a vibrator when having sex with a partner, before him. Things like that. He had me tie him to my headboard with ribbons that obviously he could have pulled lose if he wanted to. That was kind of fun.

I guess one of the hottest experiences … well, I've always liked having sex in interesting places, unusual places. Like, before I was first married we did it in the stairwell at the university when no one was around. We did it in a chiropractor's office one time when it was closed—on the exam table! We did it once on a conference room table at work.

I've had a lot of experiences that I felt were really hot so I don't feel like I'm really light on hot. I think it has to do with a sense of play and adventurousness, making something up as you go along.

Harry and I haven't done that in a while.

*** 

The most endearing habit of a lover, for me, is something I've always liked. I like it when a guy holds my face when he kisses me. That goes back to before I had sex.

I find all the ways my husband touches me to be endearing, whether we're holding hands or he's patting my rump. I'll walk by when he's without a shirt and thump his stomach. It's all playful touching and ways of letting the other one know you're there, often without saying anything. I've never been real demonstrative, in the 'I love you' saying department. I'm more likely to tell him I married him because he's the only one I can stand.

The best way to seduce me … is not to. The first time with each of my husbands, they didn't do anything, I initiated it. I probably would have refused if any of them had tried. I'm not sure why that is, but it is. I should get a high paying job as a dominatrix.

I find sloppy kissing to be the most annoying habit of guys—it's too juicy and it gets your face wet. I don't like that.

Selfishness is a real turnoff too—somebody that wants to be satisfied without wanting to give it back. What a jerk.

I hate it when a man forces my head down on his cock—the one who tries to force you into doing what he wants you to do, not what you want—that definitely comes under the category of selfish.

There have been times when Harry has come really fast but he doesn't stop there. He's a considerate lover and does whatever is necessary to make sure I have a good time too.

This may sound strange—stupid men turn me off. I don't want to have anything to do with them sexually. I don't like stupid men. My parents used to laugh at me because I'd come home from dates early and angry when my date had done something stupid.

It could be he got lost and wouldn't listen to me when I tried to tell him how to get unlost. He could have done a serious, really dumb thing or said a really dumb thing. Sex was off then—a real deal breaker. So, my first husband was a math genius. My second was a psychopath but he wasn't stupid. And of course Harry is very bright. To me, intelligence is a turn on.

There was a French guy once who wanted to get me interested in sex, so he started showing me pornography of guys with really big dicks. And it wasn't a turn on. You look at the really big dicks and think—god, he could take my tonsils out. The porno's just not attractive because there's nothing there. I put that French guy in the category of guys that just don't get it—who don't have any idea how to get a woman interested.

I also had a guy one time tell me that he could turn me on so much that I would defecate during the process. That was a real turn off. We obviously never had sex.

Sometimes erotica or porn can be good, mostly it's not. Quite frankly, the more artistic it's considered, the less I like it. I went to see Andy Warhol's movie "Trash" and I walked out in the middle. It was stupid—a hermaphrodite has a chain of sexual experiences. It was gross.

I don't care for violence either. There are some guys that have really obnoxious and violent ways of trying to turn on a woman. I don't know why they think it would work—would any woman respond to that positively?

\*\*\*

I'm fifty-six now. I would not go back to adolescence for anything. I don't know how to change the whole good girl, bad girl thing. I know that there are cultures where it doesn't exist—maybe that's a good thing.

Actually I don't really think that sex should be such a big deal. I also think that in our society little girls are sexualized way too young now. It puts too much pressure on them. Can we do both—make sex more natural, at the same time we don't force little girls to be sexual before they are ready?

Or, how can we keep little girls from having sex when they want to? Apparently I'm in that 1% for whom birth control isn't safe. Young girls won't know ahead of time if they are also. It's not enough to just inform them about birth control. A twelve year old becoming pregnant is wrong, I think. They're just too young. They need more life before trying to care for another human being.

The age I'd put it, for young girls having sex … some will be ready at twelve, some won't be ready until twenty. If a young girl wants to do it, that's fine. If she's being pressured to do it—by a guy or to be the same as her friends, then that's wrong.

***

Today, I think a good girl is somebody who's compassionate. She needs to know herself well enough to know if she's ready to have sex or not—that's compassion for herself. Young women don't have fully formed brains, they don't have control over their emotions. If she doesn't know and makes a mistake, that's not a good girl/bad girl thing.

If she's having sex for negative reasons—revenge, showing up somebody else, things that are negative—that's bad … for her. If she's doing it for positive reasons—because she cares about somebody, cares about herself, then I don't see it as bad.

The good girl/bad girl idea isn't just for young girls. Because of my mother, I don't like the terms, but basically they are universal—you apply the same criteria you would for anything else. What is your motivation for doing it? … whatever age you are.

I had a boob lift three years ago. It made a huge difference in how I felt about my breasts. I like them better. That affected my sexuality. Don't be afraid to do things that enhance sexuality. Do them.

I've learned over the years that sex, or anything else in your life, will get better as you age and become more comfortable in your own skin. The more you like yourself, the more everything will work out better.

Follow your heart. If you have strong feelings, you need to really pay attention to those feelings because they tell you something about yourself that you need to know, in order to make good decisions. Loving someone can be one of the best things we have. If emotionally you can't handle it, you need to ask for help.

Sometimes it can be chemical. There are hormonal changes, so sometimes you just get particularly horny and you may make a bad decision. You need to understand that you don't always have control. You don't have to feel guilty about chemical reactions that happen within your body.

Making a bad decision doesn't make you a bad person. There are all kinds of reasons why that could happen.

There are people who will love you unconditionally in this world—maybe in your family, maybe from outside—you need to find those people and stick with them.

# 10

# Sarah

When I was growing up in Scotland, at school, we girls definitely talked about who was a good girl and who was bad. I was always real interested in the bad girls. I wanted to know what sex really felt like.

I was the second youngest of four girls. My oldest sister created a scandal by getting pregnant when she was sixteen. My dad was pretty good about it. He didn't make her get married or go move away somewhere. Her little boy lived with us and was just part of the family. But at the time, it was quite a scandal for the family. We younger girls talked about it a lot. My parents were strict Catholics so we had to deal with all the religious stuff about sex outside marriage. All in all, my dad was pretty cool the way he handled it.

Sex itself was never really talked about, especially around the adults. Among us girls, we giggled and speculated just like all girls do. At home, my older sisters always said 'Don't do it, don't be one of the bad girls, because see what happens' ... although we all really loved my nephew.

Because of my oldest sister, and her getting pregnant when she was sixteen, I knew how babies were made but we sure didn't talk about it. We were strict Catholics. I went to a very strict Catholic high school.

At eighteen, I was really ready to go experiment for myself ... but I was scared too. I mean, I had played around but I'd never gone all the way in high school. I didn't really know anything about sex.

\*\*\*

At twenty, I let loose and started playing around. I always made sure the guy had a good time. They rarely cared whether I got off or not and I never pushed it. It didn't seem as important as the snuggling and kissing and affection that you get sometimes.

Well, I continued to play around for awhile, but not with a whole lot of guys. I got married at twenty-three. My husband had a high sex drive and wanted to do it every night, often several times a night.

After awhile, I wasn't even beginning to get enough sleep, but I faked getting off and put up with it for years. Finally, I told him I didn't want to do it every night, I needed some sleep. And since I really wasn't getting off, I wanted to slow the sex way down with him.

By that time, the two girls were growing up and I went to work. Eventually I had a good job, a nice circle of friends and I started to feel good about myself. I was tired of him and I wanted more freedom, more affection. We decided to get divorced. Just after we started the paperwork, he was diagnosed with cancer.

Boy, I had to think long and hard about that. Finally, I decided to stay with him through his illness, but not as man and wife. I didn't want to have sex with him anymore.

It was several years before he finally passed on. It was hard but I'm glad I did it. It was good for both me and my girls, even though it really was hard on all of us. I strayed only once during that time. I knew a man who was older, but he was very nice and supportive. He was affectionate and gentle with me, really made me feel good. One night, I kind of snuck out to his car, sitting in front of our house. We sat there for a long time. I cried and he held me gently. I really liked that. Eventually we made love. It was nice.

***

My husband died two years ago and I've been free to experiment sexually since then. I'm having a really great time. Party, party! Just recently I met a new man, Bill, from the States, and we've fallen in love. I'm leaving here in a few days and going to live with him. I don't know what will happen but we're really good together and we laugh a lot.

I still don't orgasm much but occasionally I've had a lover who cares enough to take the time to get me there. I'm beginning to think that maybe it's time to open myself up to really going deeper with a man, you know, in a relationship. Bill takes his time when we make love and it is REALLY great. But I don't get off every time. Maybe I can actually do that—share deeper from within myself with him.

The island guys have been fun. I love the sensualness of their dark skin against my white skin. I just really love looking at that. They are pretty good lovers—we laugh a lot. That's what makes it good for me. It's really important that we can laugh together. It has to be fun. I don't let any of them get all that serious or think it's going to last very long. They will move on to someone younger and more serious. I make 'em wear a rubber. I mean, what if they got it on with some girl who had a disease? And then took it home? He doesn't know me. And I don't know him. Wear a rubber!

I've only played with one married man. I don't really like to do that.

\*\*\*

For me, the good girl is the one who doesn't get caught. All of us usually agreed at school who the bad girls were—the boys talked about them. I always wanted to know what they knew—you know, like what did it actually feel like to have sex?

Personally I didn't worry about good girl/bad girl. My oldest sister had been the bad girl and I still loved her and definitely loved her son. So I saw myself as a good girl with a lot of curiosity. I mean, there's nothing bad about sex, as long as both people want to—that can't be good or bad. But I think it's really bad when someone tries to force another person. Now that's bad.

I talked to my daughters about sex. I told them all about their periods being natural and not nasty. And being responsible for their own sexing. Later, when I tried to talk to them, they'd already gotten the details in school. The older one told the younger one. Then when I tried to talk to them, they said 'Mom, we know all that already. Go away.'

I could tell when my oldest started having sex, so I asked her. She didn't want to talk about it but I asked about protection and she said she had it covered. They made it clear they weren't going to tell me anything else, so go away Mom!

I will say something. The thing was, during the divorce, they kept asking me why I was so serious. So sad. They said 'You're doing the right thing, Mom,' but I didn't want to tell them I was having an affair. They knew anyhow. And it turned out good because we were close enough that they could see that I was still a woman. It made the whole thing much easier.

That's the thing—my kids are open with me, we talk about these things. Some of their boyfriends say, 'oh, you're going to talk to your mom.' 'Yes!'

They check in with me, too. I had problems with one boyfriend and they were willing to go and sort him out. 'I can do it on my own,' I said. 'No, we're going to sort him out, you need some help.' They could see my face. 'We're going to tell him, yes we are.'

Mothers and daughters—now they are women so we can women-talk. It's funny bouncing it back in their court. As mom, I always asked them what was wrong. Now they do it to me too. So it's okay, even if it's me doing something wrong. It was really a turning point in their lives. 'Come on, guys, I'm a woman. I can make mistakes.' It made us bond so much better.

We've lost a bit of the bond, now that the older one is married. Just a bit, but we can talk about almost anything with each other. He's (her husband) actually quite jealous. He doesn't leave our side for five minutes, in case we're talking about him.

A lot of people are jealous of our bond, so they're saying to me now. Then the guys try to say to the girls, 'I'm your one and only, I should be in charge of you.'

\*\*\*

I've had a good time playing with a bunch of different lovers in the last two years, since my husband died. But since I've met Bill, I am beginning to think differently. I think I'm a good lover, in that I always make sure he has a good time and gets what he wants. I laugh and have a good time, make him feel like he's the best to be around. I never make a guy feel guilty because I don't get off. Actually, I fake it a lot so they won't know. It's just easier that way. I really enjoy affection and snuggling the most anyhow, so why not fake the orgasm? They'll never know.

I never thought about deliberately exploring myself sexually. It's an interesting thought. I mean, I always have focused on making sure the guy has a good time. Yeah, I masturbate sometimes and then I almost always get off, have an orgasm. But really exploring myself? I've never even thought about doing that.

But I might. It would be fun to be more open with Bill. I really do trust him sexually, more than I have with anybody else. Could be fun! Bill is a really nice guy. We laugh all the time when we're together and we have a great time. I'm a little nervous about just taking off and moving to the States. It'll be my first time there.

We only met four days before he had to leave here—the island—but we spent all our time together because we just connected right away. It just feels so perfect. I'm scared but I'm going to do it, go up there. And maybe be more open about getting what I want out of it. You know, talking about sex and taking our relationship to a deeper level.

Bill makes me feel so good. I feel safe and protected and connected with him, like we've known each several lifetimes already. This has been really good, talking about this with you, because I think I could open myself up more with him. We just are so good together. Plus I'm older now. I guess it's time I let myself be real with someone.

My experience of sex has changed over the years in that I used to never expect anything from the guy. I mean, I had fun but the guys didn't seem to care whether I got off or not. They only cared if they did. So I put my attention on them, their pleasure. If they were nice guys, and usually they are, I just decided that that was going to be fun enough too. I've had sex with a lotta guys now and Bill is different. I could see being with him for the rest of my life.

\*\*\*

My hottest fantasy? Well, laughing a lot is part of it. Getting it on with the really dark black men around here has been a very hot fantasy for a long time. What's my current favorite fantasy? Let me think if I have one!

It's hard to say what has been my hottest experience. I mean, it's all about affection, isn't it? Touching and being touched. I took on a really younger guy recently. He just didn't know what to do. He touched a little here and there but then finally I took over. It was fun having a younger guy be interested in me. I got to be the older woman, right? That was fun.

And so I started kissing him, all over his body. I guess no one had ever done that to him. With this guy I was totally in control. They're just so lost, the young ones. They lie there … like babies almost … and you do nothing aside from touching and kissing. I find that funny—I couldn't stop myself from laughing half the time.

See—that's sex—fingers, mouth, touch, kiss—you don't even have to do anything else. You can get them to the point where it feels so good that it's enough, even without intercourse.

Afterwards I told him that if he just did the same things to his girlfriend, she would love it. He said he thought he was going to be a much better lover now and thanked me.

The process is the fun. The young ones need to learn that. So I think women have to cross their ego borders, now and again, to let men know what we want them to do. Otherwise, you're gonna have one short night. It'll be like we're making out, haven't even done nothing as far as I'm concerned and he's already gone off. He needs to learn about that, minimally.

We can all go for the wham bam occasionally, but you need to know some things, have some skills, if you want to be a good lover. Like I know when I'm touching a man that this is gonna work, and I know that is gonna work. And if they don't work, hey that's okay, I'll try in another direction.

You have to know yourself and your own body. Then share it with someone. It's nice with the young ones because they're more willing to learn. We have fun. Then ten minutes later we get to have fun some more! Ah, the young ones.

What I don't like about sex is when there's no affection. I need to laugh in order to just be me, to relax. If he makes me uptight or nervous, I'm outta there. I don't like hitting and hard stuff.

I'm sure there are some things I won't do. I'm not into bondage stuff … I'm gonna try it though. Something about another person being in charge of me, that's hard. I can't see me really getting into it. I could probably be the dominatrix. It's important to me to be equal. But, never say never.

I've had anal sex in the last two years, twice. That's something really new for me. I wasn't sure about it but I wanted to try it. If you don't like, you don't like it, I figured. I wanted to know if I liked it or not … I still don't know. Probably it is because I wasn't feeling completely safe with the man. It was okay … but I think if I felt completely safe with someone I might enjoy it. You gotta trust them. And I was worried about my own cleanliness. I hadn't cleaned myself out, didn't know what I was doing. I couldn't relax.

The absolutely most annoying habit guys have that I just HATE, is when they push my head and mouth down on their cocks. Push me? I don't like it at all. The angle is usually wrong and I get a hard cock jammed backwards down my throat. I don't like it. When a guy does that, I make him leave or I leave.

Guys come up to you at a bar and you get interested, but the ones who want to go right away and jump into bed are boring. I want a man to dance with me first. Laugh and dance with me if they want to get into bed with me. That's all.

And I don't like it when a guy expects from me, you know, like he just expects I'm going to want to make out with him. Guys are weird sometimes. I want dancing and laughing and affection before sex—that's what counts for me.

What I really like most about sex is that affection that hopefully comes with it. I'm used to not getting off, so laughing together and touching each other, snuggling, kissing, you know—affection—these are important to me. The older I get, the more that's what I want. I mean, you can only have sex so many times and you can always touch each other affectionately.

I like afterwards, the cuddling. I love that a lot. To me, to spend the whole night together, that is the best.

Anticipation is really good too—then it's fun twice. Sex is not serious. It doesn't have to be. One guy, my Copan lover, was a total 'wham bam thank you ma'am'… but I was completely desperate that night. Finally I went, 'Whoa, I'm outa here.' But what are you going to do?

When I get to the States, it's gonna be okay. Because I love him the same way he feels about me, so I can just go there and chill out. It'll be okay. I don't want any kind of fuss.

The most endearing habits around sex all come back to the same things. Laughter, affection, dancing together. Those are what make it fun for me. Anything he does—touching my shoulder as he passes, looking at me special. Some men have intelligence about touching, all they have to do is touch you and … wow.

***

Sexually, nothing much has changed for me before and after menopause. I'm kinda in the middle of it. Except, I seem to have this higher sex drive now. For sure, I'm having more fun. And now with Bill, I can hardly believe how lucky I am. It's a whole new life.

See, I really hadn't thought much about a lot of these things before. Now I can think about them and I could change everything, like loosening up inside and getting closer. Well, we'll see.

Looking back, I don't think I was ever really a bad girl. I never deliberately hurt anyone, and that's what bad is. How can anything else be bad? Yes, it's hard when a teenage girl gets pregnant, but it isn't bad.

***

To my daughters and granddaughters—first of all, let it be fun. At the same time, always remain your own person. Make sure somebody else doesn't take you over. Do what you want.

And once you're past that stage a little bit, then it's about love and affection. Look for it, don't just bounce them off, one after another. Actually, you don't even have to go looking for it, you just have to be open for it. Be nice to one another.

Play with someone and keep playing with him and it will get better. Fulfill yourself—that's okay—and you're alright to be who you are. Then be a good partner, a joint equal partner. Don't lose your self-esteem. If it doesn't work, at least you gave it your best. It's all you can do.

# 11

# Eva

I was in a girl's school for high school, and we definitely had a lot of good girl/bad girl training—mostly from each other. There was one girl who was considered really bad, KO, but when I look back I think it was more the persona she put on. Maybe she was sexually active but she wasn't close to me so I never heard her actually say that. Good girls definitely weren't supposed to do it, look like they were doing it ... or talk slutty either.

The rest of us were looking to get kissed ... if we were lucky, maybe have a boyfriend for some serious petting. I was younger than my classmates, so my experience with boys, and my awareness of things, was a lot less.

But I had learned about masturbating and did a lot of that in high school. I would study and read with one hand in my panties ... almost always. I played with myself all the time.

That's when I learned about orgasms, lots of orgasms. How delicious! Getting off was my reason for being from then on. After awhile, I discovered I could prolong the orgasm and just kind of float there ... peak as much as I had time for, without being finished. If I rushed to an orgasm, I was finished. If I went slow, I could have all the orgasms I wanted. It was fun.

When I graduated from high school, at sixteen, I didn't know any boys. I did neck once in my senior year, with a friend of a friend. It was quite very delicious.

Even in college, boys seemed like alien creatures to me. I was chubby and none of them noticed me. Since I'd been playing with myself for so long, I learned to move sexual energy out of my genitals and around my body. Three days before my eighteenth birthday, I finally gave up my cherry to some guy I'd met at a party. A definite one night stand. I sure didn't have a clue what I was supposed to do and it was over fast. When I asked for more, he said he couldn't. It wasn't very fun.

\*\*\*

I remember being five years old and hiding in the bathroom at the corner gas station with two boys my age. I dropped my pants and we were playing at sticking his thing in me when a woman came in, screeched at us and ran out. We ran away fast. I don't know where I knew about putting his thing in me.

Sex was never ever talked about when I was growing up. I learned whatever I learned on my own. I remember being in fifth grade—I'd gone to the local branch library and snuck into the section that had medical books. I saw pictures of all kinds of the strangest deformities in those books, and also finally learned the word *penis* and saw pictures of them—erect, flaccid, deformed, all kinds. I went to school the next day feeling like I'd discovered the Rosetta stone. I told my girlfriends about it and we tittered for days and days.

Several of us actually formed a little club—we would get together for a sleep over, then quietly partner up and play with each other's clitoris, sometimes late into the night. I don't remember ever having an orgasm during those sessions, but it always felt good—both touching and being touched. We took turns. This went on into junior high school but petered out by eighth grade.

At home, I had a father and brother but had never seen a penis—that girls and boys were different was never acknowledged, except that we weren't ever supposed to be undressed around each other.

My mom and older sister never told me about my period either. When I finally started having a period, one of them put a box of Kotex and one of those weird belts in my room. Not a word was spoken about it.

Like I said, just before my eighteen birthday, I lost my virginity. I didn't feel like one of the bad girls, but I felt like I won something by actually losing my cherry while I was still 'jail bait.' I had been Miss Goodie-two-shoes at home but wanted to be just a little bit the bad girl.

I knew I was obsessed with sex. I wanted more all the time. I wanted to learn everything I could while at the same time still look like a good girl. It was 1966 and free love hadn't made it into our thinking yet. I hadn't smoked any pot yet either.

Underneath, I thought sex was bad and I was bad for enjoying it so much. I didn't question much then. I had to sneak the masturbating for sure. I didn't begin to really understand women's liberation for a long time.

In my family, my father was in charge—no question. I was the youngest of three children and precocious. I decided that I would imitate my father, instead of my mother, because he had the power, the money, the leather strap, the scathing, superior-acting sarcasm. I wanted to be powerful, like him, but without being abusive.

When I was growing up, my father would whip me with his big leather belt if I laughed too much, giggling or whatever. Then my older brother would beat me up for crying about it. I learned it was dangerous to laugh or cry, so I decided I'd be brainy instead ... then everybody seemed to hate me. Oh, well. Later I went to a shrink and he seemed to think I had all the characteristics of a sexually abused child, but I don't remember anything like that.

My mother endured—she put up with his outrages, neither protecting herself nor us. Why would I want to be like her, I thought? It was years before I understood that I had power through my sexuality—that I could say no to a guy without feeling guilty.

My dad had made it pretty clear that I should be grateful to any bozo who put any attention on me at all. But the attention my father and brother put on me hadn't been much fun, so I really wasn't hurrying to have a man in my life. I got fat instead, which worked pretty good at keeping the boys away. Even when I started putting out a lot.

Like most young people, I didn't worry about getting pregnant either—only because it couldn't happen to me, right? The Pill was fairly available when I was in college, so I availed myself of it.

The People's Park protests started right down the street from where I lived, and I joined the protests against the 'pigs' and the Viet Nam war. Then it was the 70s and everything changed again. I remember the 70s mostly because they followed what I thought of as just an awful time—Viet Nam, the assassinations of JFK, ML King, Bobby—I was a teenage girl trying to make sense of the world, surrounded by riots and shootings and burnings. Peace and openness and free love seemed like the right antidote to all of it. I was thankful I had lived through it.

God, we thought we knew it all. And a lot of it we did—peace, love—very basic simple stuff. At sixty years old, now, it still resonates with me 'Practice loving kindness toward yourself'—that could be the wisest thing anybody ever said.

I soon became an experienced enough lover to be aware of who was a good lover and who was a bad lover. I had longer relationships with two different Jims at the same time. One of them was enthusiastic, always ready, made me feel wanted. We had a really good time together. The other was older, separated from his wife, a doctoral student in chemistry. He was just absolutely hot to me. But I was younger and had to pursue him a bit. I loved making love with him because he took his time, focused on me. I felt ... acknowledged in the process.

By the mid-70s, beyond the Jims, despite the so-called sexual revolution, I was tired of guys who weren't really interested in my pleasure, in the sense that they didn't know anything about my body except where to stick their dicks. It was very hit or miss about getting off. I loved to orgasm. I had spent many many hours in my teens rubbing on myself and I knew I could come for a very long time, just hanging there in a beautiful orgasmic ... not void ... but almost nether world. Except it never seemed to be that way when I was with a lover *and* I wanted it to be better than that with a lover. I was sure it was my fault, too.

I also really loved intercourse. I loved cock—in all my holes. But very few men have any kind of finesse or understanding of foreplay. Most men thought it was a first date thing they never had to do again. I had been so programmed by my father to never question or correct a man that it didn't occur to me to talk to my partner about my body or sexuality.

Well, that doesn't really sound like what it was. I had a high sex drive, but even then it was about quality. I slept with a lot of guys during the early 70s, hoping to find 'the one.' Most of the time, I just wasn't being fully satisfied, without foreplay, and the time to reach even close to my full potential. So I was constantly undercomed and often horny and bitchy about it.

\*\*\*

In 1974, I met Fred. Later I married him. He was a lot older than me and as interested in quality sex as I was. We took a bunch of sex classes together and for the first time, I had the experience of consistently coming better with him than alone. I was amazed that people talked about sex in groups, that people had been studying sex for centuries. I knew then I had a lifetime of delicious learning in front of me.

Sometimes, I went way way out, to what I called 'riding the filament'—it's as high as I ever get on sex—a wonderful place of riding an energy wave that is all pure energy and void at the same time. We don't really have the words in English. Yum.

We did a method called ecstatic childbirth when my first child was born. Something changed in me. Riding the filament became an experience of the Universal Energy then. I hadn't thought much about God, except to know I didn't believe in organized religions, and I didn't know to call it a higher state of consciousness at that time. Sex became very sacred to me, a pure and authentic place ... unlike the messiness the rest of my life became.

I left him when he left me for his boyfriend. But I was used to coming for hours at a time. We had trained him to extended orgasm also, so coming for hours was a way of life for us. We had been mostly monogamous, but towards the end we each had other partners from within the group who had taken the same classes as us.

I felt so betrayed that I wouldn't have anything to do with those people when my husband and I divorced. I still thought I could only get way out there sexually with a partner, so I substituted quantity for quality ... but that didn't last long. I was very frustrated by what I saw as the total sexual immaturity of the American male in the 80s. They didn't want to learn—that seemed childish to me.

I had been so disappointed by so many bad lovers that I wasn't interested in men anymore. For awhile I thought I might be a lesbian, but I realized the issue wasn't gender, it was awareness, or lack of it on a partner's side. I wanted to protect that sacred place and not share it with bozos just because they had a willie between their legs ... that they didn't know how to use!

***

I studied Taoist sexology and Tantra. Sexual energy became the pathway to deeper awareness for me—a sacred journey I was willing to take by myself if I had to. It has involved keeping my body healthy as I've aged ... clearing and healing and cleaning out—purifying the stuff from my childhood and going beyond that to a more joyful state of being.

Now I'm pretty much celibate, comfortable with my body and skilled at channeling sexual energy where and when I want it. Now, though, I also want cuddling, affection, something else. A companion and friend to play with would be nice.

I turned sixty last year. I have more years behind me than in front of me. All the choices of life's living that hassle us as we raise families and create careers—I'm all done with that. I'm hoping these really will be the golden years for me. I would prefer doing it with a partner ... I think ... sometimes.

Lots of people used to call me a man-hater and a 'lesbo' but I'm neither of those things. I just won't submit my body and happiness to a man who's a closet woman-hater. It's not the same thing at all.

Frankly, I've felt all my life like parents, family, friends and partners have beaten me up, punished me for having a high sex drive. People tried to take my children away, saying I was sick for enjoying breast-feeding, that I had no maternal instincts because I enjoyed sex too much. I hated men for awhile. Then, for the sake of my own sanity, I forgave them. I still don't trust men much, though.

So there I was, with a high sex drive, committed to quality sex and without a partner who could take me there ... and a fair amount of fear about revealing my true nature anymore. I eventually came to a deeper understanding of the concept of karma ... so now I figure it differently.

I was young and in the middle of the free love revolution, which seemed at the time like it was only about getting off for the guys. Few men are interested in quality sex ... few women too, judging by my experiences. In many ways, I had the best of it—great ecstasy training when I was young and then the freedom to pursue whatever I wanted to. That a man might want to take care of me? Hasn't ever happened, although I think it would be nice.

\*\*\*

From my humble perspective, a good girl is the one who is true to herself. It has nothing to do with what's going on 'out there.' And that will be different for every girl. I mean, who is to say that it isn't good to experiment with a lot of different men? Who is to say it isn't good to be monogamous for fifty years? Who of us really knows what's good for another person? Most people don't take the time to even figure out what's true about themselves!

A 'bad' girl, well I'd have to define a bad girl as someone who lies to herself about who she is and what she wants to do with her body. It's only when she lies to herself that she's bad. I'm not saying this very well. Bad is when you're withholding or wasting your unique special energy in the world. A bad girl hurts herself and others when she does that. A bad girl wastes herself by choosing not to learn about herself.

I think I've been both good and bad—all mixed up over the years. I quit sex for awhile because I felt like I was drawing men to me who were totally unconscious and I *felt* bad after sex with them—like I had allowed myself to be poorly used. I've never been into forcing anything on anybody else, so I'm not bad that way.

But, I have tried to use sex to get things, to manipulate and control men—honestly I was never very good at it. I've known lots of women who went from marriage to marriage getting richer and richer. Part of me envies them, part of me exults in the freedoms I've had—adventures all over the place.

During one particularly harsh period, I became a call girl in order to make good money, which I needed to pay off a lawyer. I had a day job, a weekend job and then a night job. I ended up doing a lot of calls for disabled Viet Nam vets who were house bound and needed some relief. I actually felt pretty righteous about that—at least it was honest help and I didn't feel sleazy.

The last lover I had, about three years ago, was a highly educated architect turned Ph.D. psychotherapist, who was—he professed often and loudly—deeply involved in a spiritual path and understanding himself.

He *did* know where my clitoris is, I'll give him that. But he was totally out of his body every time we made love. He would begin to rub on me, close his eyes and go off into some fantasy world. I come really easily, so each of the two times we made love and I hit the first peak, he stopped touching me and started humping. I couldn't get him to kiss me, or look at me, or touch me during intercourse, like it was only about his getting off as quickly as possible. It was all friction. Boring . . . and very typical. I had hoped intelligent guys at least had figured it out.

I don't mind if a man doesn't know anything significant about his own sexuality or mine ... as long as he has some desire to learn more. Most men, even at our age, still have their egos all tied up in their cocks and seem afraid to learn anything about sex from a woman. How very odd that seems to me.

I think I'm a good lover. I really like touching another person, getting in tune with his energy. I like to take my time being aroused and arousing his whole body. Sucking on a cock really turns me on. I love the feel of the skin over a hard cock, juices, the hardness itself. So I get my jollies whatever he does, as long as he's in his body and actually feeling it.

If he's off in a fantasy or thinking about his performance or something else, there's no pleasure there for me. I want a partner interested in seeing how much further we can take it, together.

***

I've always been exploring myself sexually—every minute of my life from adolescence on. Somehow nothing else has ever seemed as important to understand and honor, as if sex is *the* gift from the Universe. I mean, here is this body with these parts and pieces that are designed for pleasure. To me, that means that pleasure is important to being human.

I tried to be responsible sexually, even in the midst of my high libido. How do you focus on your own pleasure and still be functional, compassionate and involved in the world? I did my best, which included retreating from the sexual arena completely when it wasn't working for me.

I've certainly paid heavily in life for following that path. The legal system, my family, even partners, have all come after me, treating me like I was a 'bad' woman—and even a criminal—because I had a high libido. I thought sex was important and I was willing to talk about it. They seemed to think I was dangerous. It just made me more determined to understand it.

I was raped twice, for having the audacity to say no to a guy. Combined with the physical abuse from my father and brother, I don't trust men very much, even after years of therapy and processing. I guess that's my cross to bear this lifetime.

I know people from those times, who later came to me when they had sexual problems, asking me to help them fix it. Our society is so skewed when it comes to sex.

One of the problems with exploring your own sexuality, especially for a woman, is that it's hard to find your own limits. For instance, guys work really hard to orgasm quickly, then fall asleep like they've lost all their energy. Women can come for hours and be rejuvenated by it. So how much of a woman's time *should* she spend finding out what her limits really are, if any? And if your partner doesn't care, isn't interested in having you come that much better than he does, do you stop exploring yourself or change the partner? Which way is truer to yourself?

I was lucky it was so good with my husband for those years. We trained his body to extended orgasms too. He could come and come and come and never get off, even in his late forties.

During my single years, I really wanted the closeness, snuggling and affection of a partner, but even guys who understood that need in me didn't have a clue about a woman's *capacity* for going into her body and mastering the energy running through it. They couldn't ever seem to *satisfy* me sexually. And it got to the point where staying open, staying on, without ever getting *filled*, became painful. It just got easier to not bother with a partner.

Now I get off, or come, as much as I want and it doesn't matter if there is a partner who does or doesn't do something. He is not in charge of either my turn on or my pleasure. Nothing outside of me is. I am in charge of what I feel, and when. Always. I get lonely occasionally, but less as I get older. I'm very comfortable with myself.

***

Well, I've already talked about how my experience of sex has changed over the years. I was obsessed as a teenager and through my twenties and thirties. I had one relationship for several years in my forties, and a fucking buddy during my fifties. The rest of the time I've been celibate and okay with that. Like I said before, I'm considering a partner as a possibility again.

From another perspective, my experience of sex has changed in that I started from lots of masturbating and orgasms, to long sessions of just floating beyond orgasms, to eventually coming all the time. I lost some of that capacity during menopause, mostly because my hormones were chaotic for awhile. Now I'm interested again, feeling sexy and willing.

I've probably had sex with 200 men over the last 40+ years. I've experimented in every way I could envision, including bisexual stuff, swingers stuff, group orgies, you name it, I tried it—except for heavy s&m. I wish I could have done it all with one partner, but that wasn't the way life worked out for me.

Who knows why it works out one way or another. It just did. I figure I've got about thirty years left so maybe I'll meet a good guy and we can spend our golden years coming a whole lot. That would be fun!

***

For years and years, when I had fantasies, my favorite was some variation on being out in a peaceful meadow surrounded by trees, really private and wild. I would be lying on a blanket under an old oak tree, with dappled summer sunlight playing across my naked body. As I begin rubbing on myself, getting closer and closer to heavy coming, a shadow crosses the sunlight. Etcetera, etcetera. Stranger, no talking, great sex, no bullshit.

My fantasy has changed recently. Now I dream about a partner who wants to dance with me. He wears silk pajama bottoms, I wear something silky and sensual. He's in charge of the music and always chooses two or three pieces that build me up. He takes me in his arms and we dance fast and slow. My nipples rub against his bare chest. His cock slips between my legs and we keep dancing—tango, maybe. We kiss sometimes, looking deeply at each other. Then we go to our bed, fully connected and panting for each other.

I don't ever fantasize with a live partner. Sometimes I do enjoy the fantasy I just spoke of when I'm self-pleasuring—it gets me going, jumpstarts my turn on. I also use a biofeedback technique I learned about twenty-five years ago. It doesn't take much jumpstarting or fantasies, I just go totally into the actual sensations of my body, but sometimes I fantasize for the fun of it.

It would be very hard for me to decide which was my hottest experience. I've had many and after the high sex training, I've trained myself to allow each time to be better than the last. So my hottest experience is the next one and the one after that! Nonetheless …

It definitely wasn't the group sex or swinger stuff. I'd say it was one time with a friend who just took hours taking me up as high as I've ever gone. We never had intercourse that night, he just focused on taking me way way out there and he was tuned in enough to go out there with me. That I think is as good as it's ever gotten for me. I rode the filament that night for hours and hours. I love riding the filament together.

What I like most about sex is sharing affection, the feeling of being connected, being one with another person. High sex does that. All I can equate it to is an ecstatic experience of Source, God, Great Spirit, pure energy, whatever you want to call it. That feeling that you have transcended this physical space and time dimension and tuned into significantly higher frequencies. I come out of it totally at peace with myself and the world and just naturally joyful about life.

I won't kid you, though, what I like the most—a lot—is coming. I love to come. I love the sheer physicality of sex—juices, smells, sounds, lips and hair and lots of skin. I love it when some animal instinctual nature takes me over and all I can do is rub my nipples on his chest, suck and nibble and bite his neck. I love putting my face in his crotch, smelling and tasting him. I enjoy nuzzling a soft cock. I really love that sensation when his cock first slowly enters me. I love it when I'm moved to laughter and tears by the overwhelming intimacy of what we've just shared, as if we had created something of beauty in the universe.

What I like least about sex is how men just want to get off fast. What a waste! And when they carry their macho controlling bullshit into my bed and want to be in charge, it really turns me off. Most men aren't willing to allow a woman to know more than them because it threatens their tender egos, or they aren't willing to consider learning something new—those guys are really boring lovers.

I mean, I understand that there's no point in making judgments about people who don't know any better. I just choose not to be around them anymore. I don't mean to sound like a snob or a ball buster. But guys aren't going to become better lovers if women don't ever tell them they have a lot to learn. How do you learn otherwise?

I also dislike, as in get really bored with, sexing when you're laying down. I mean, who says you have to be flat on a bed … all the time? What about sitting up and touching? And then there's the shortcut maneuver around foreplay—'Just lay down, I'll suck on you.' Yeah, I appreciate the sentiment, but it's not enough to just touch the tip of my clit with the tip of his tongue. It's just not near enough connection to really warm me up. I need much larger sections of my skin touched by much larger sections of his skin. Let's do a 69-type position on our sides so most of our bodies are touching. That works to get me ready for intercourse.

I've waited years for the chance to talk about some of this. I hope some guys actually read it and get it … for all the women out there who are like me.

In terms of sexual acts, I've done it all except, as I said, s&m stuff. I'm not into pain as the path to pleasure.

The most annoying habit of men that I've experienced is forcing my head down on their cocks for a blowjob. Give me a break. How totally 50s, yet lots of guys still think that's cool. I think it must come from adolescence and male control fantasies because it sure isn't comfortable for a woman.

The most endearing habits of a lover, as far as I'm concerned, all have to do with keeping the energy moving between us when we're not in bed. Affection, in all the little and big ways that a partner can create it. I truly believe that men are naturally more romantic than women.

I can easily be swept off my feet by a man who does something to let me know he thinks about me when he's not with me, whether it's as simple as doing the dishes before I get home, bringing flowers, running a bath, placing his hand on my shoulder—there's no way to make a list of all the things that could come under the label of affection.

During menopause, I pretty much lost all interest in sex. My vaginal juices dried up. My desire for sex and a relationship went totally away. But now, the years have passed and that itch, that tingle, is coming back. Now I feel more like a 'real' woman than at any other time in my life—in the sense of being free to really explore myself beyond a gender role.

\*\*\*

Well, the years have passed, so what have I learned about good and bad? Mostly that there isn't such a thing. I mean, if good means being true to yourself, then bad is ... what? Being unconscious or neurotic? Where's the compassion for oneself and others in judgment? I know I said before that bad girls don't develop themselves.

John Lennon said it best—'Life is what happens when you're busy making plans.' Always learning is what counts the most.

My life has really changed over the last years. I wasn't interested in sex during menopause. I stopped having 'an orgasm a day.' It was a dark time for me, like a momma bear in her winter cave. At the same time, it was filled with 'babies'—seeds germinating in the dark. I brought some clarity to toxic stuff from the first fifty years. Some of those seeds are sprouting into wonderful new adventures now.

I do believe there is a partner somewhere out there for me, for the next thirty years. I feel stronger and hopeful again. I'm bringing my 'powers' online again—talents and blessings I had shut off when I got so angry at men.

I have two wonderful grown children and one new grandchild. I can change the future for her ... make it better ... by staying healthy, positive and active. Maybe that's a little bit of wisdom.

Things like making money, caring what someone else thinks about how I look, all that stuff—it just doesn't matter—it never did except in my head. I'm calmer. I listen better. I actually finish things. I hope finishing this life includes finding a friend/lover/partner who gets it about women and sex.

***

My final words to daughters and granddaughters everywhere? Be true to your own sexual nature, AND, that will take time, by yourself, to figure out. Just you and your body, finding out how it all works, before you take on a partner because otherwise you're more likely to give yourself up ... and then it's harder to find yourself again. Dildos and vibrators are okay except they will dull your nerve endings and in the long run make it harder to feel the prolonged ecstatic states. Well ... non-mechanical dildos can fill a need sometimes ... hmmmm.

In sex, go for quality because quantity isn't worth the effort. Actually experiencing yourself as pure energy is worth every ounce of effort. It will make your life your own ... and more.

It doesn't matter what anyone else says they think about what you do. Define your values for yourself—what really matters to you and what a 'good' life looks like *for you*—and then love yourself enough to live by them.

# 12

# Stephanie

I went to an all-girls Catholic school. There was tittering about good girls and bad girls, but it wasn't about me, it was always about someone else. The girls who had the biggest breasts, they got the most abuse. But it wasn't me.

We defined the bad girl as someone who kissed, say in grammar school, and in high school would go all the way. That's basically how bad girls were defined—girls that would go all the way. We included girls that were interested in sex and the most developed girls. Whereas, I wasn't interested in sex at all. It didn't faze me one way or another.

I remember when I was sixteen years old, that was the year my friends and I started to get curious about sex. We were juniors in high school. Up until then, we just hung around and played. We played Barbie dolls, or we played sports or other things. We knew there were those 'bad' girls, but my group just wasn't involved in it at all. I guess we were innocent.

My mother to this day still hasn't talked about sex, or periods for that matter. And fathers never talk to daughters about sex. We just didn't talk about it. Never. My mom used to send me to the corner drug store, when there was a real druggist in a little corner store. She handed me a little piece of paper that said Kotex on it and I would hand it to him and he would give me a box. But I had never thought of what it was for. I just knew every once in a while I'd have a little slip to give him and he gave me a package to take back to her.

I tried my girls in that conversation, and they'd go 'Oh, Mom, too much information. I just asked you … yes or no.' I guess no one really wants to hear about it from their parents. My kids just asked specific questions, nothing else.

In college, I had a lot of boyfriends, a lot. In my senior year of high school, I started going out with this one guy. He expected—we both expected—to get married. I dated him exclusively for four years. At some point, though, I thought ... no, I don't think he's 'the one.'

When I was twenty, I just went berserk. I made up for lost time. I started thinking about other boys and looking for the right guy. I wanted to be accepted by someone that I picked, not who picked me. I dated a lot. I liked to go out with a lot of guys and have a good time.

I never really had another serious relationship during that time. I would date for a couple of weeks and then toss him aside. I'd have two dates in one day.

I had a lot of other things on my plate too. I was going to school, I was working fulltime. I didn't have too much time to think about it. Then I came out to California.

I never really was happy in New York—I always knew that was not where I wanted to stay. So any relationships I would get involved in, I always knew that wasn't where I was going to be. Relationships weren't going to last because I was leaving.

It was a sexual revolution. The Pill had just come out. Now we could have sex all we wanted. If we got a sexual disease, penicillin would kill it, so we could have multiple partners. I was always a little more detached, though, because that wasn't where I was going to be and what I was going to do.

***

I came to California to visit a girlfriend and never went back. But I was always really career oriented. I had a job on Wall Street and went to school full time—I didn't have too much time to play.

I had a career in accounting out here too. I dated a lot of guys, probably with the same enthusiasm as in New York. Then I met Ben and I've been completely monogamous since then. We've been together thirty-two years.

I have to say, sex didn't really interest me. I was more interested in the person. The kindness, the personality, sense of humor, how he looked—to me those things were more important. I always looked for personalty ... temperament. If the sex was compatible also, that was nice.

I grew up in a home where my mother and my father never fought. I never saw or heard them fight once in my whole life. And that's kind of the person I was going for—mellow, so my life could be pretty much like that.

***

I told you this was going to be boring, me being monogamous for thirty-two years. It's not that I don't look at other guys ... but, I don't. If he's really handsome, that's nice, but just because he's attractive doesn't mean I want to bed him down. I can say I've only had two monogamous relationships—one at the beginning of my sexuality lasting four years, and one at the end of my sexuality lasting thirty-two years.

Sexually, it's not been dissatisfying. It was never a big issue with me. I have low estrogen perhaps—to me that's normal. I just was never a very sexual person. I don't wear a bathing suit, I don't like to be naked and I don't like massages because I don't like strangers touching me. I just don't like it. So ergo, monogamy is easy ... way easy.

I do orgasm regularly ... all the time. So it's been satisfying.

If we have a choice—to take a nap or make love, today we take a nap. But that's about all that's changed. We can make an adult decision to nap first and it's not insulting to either one of us. Nothing fundamental has changed.

Actually we're both satisfied, I'd like to think. When we were first married, we actually tried to have kids. I'm not sure I really wanted to get married, but my Catholic upbringing ... you get married in order to have kids. So once we decided we would have kids, we got married.

Then they told me I could never have children, so I had a hysterectomy. I had endometriosis. As the anesthesia started to wear off, rather than complete the surgery, they left some of my organs there. I had one ovary left. Shortly after that I got pregnant with Sheila—I had, like, minimal parts! Nine months later I was pregnant again, with Audrey, so then they finished taking the rest of my organs out.

So I'm really blessed because I went from not really knowing if I wanted to be married, to having two children. God works in mysterious ways. Early on, we tried and tried to have kids but my insides were rotten. The doctor said it wasn't ever going to happen, so we decided we would adopt. We were going to have U.N. babies—a little black baby and a little Chinese baby—just adopt everybody. And then I got pregnant.

***

I hate to blow your study about sexuality and I don't want to say that I don't have any sexuality. It's just that it's not cool, it embarrasses me. It's kind of a personal thing and it's supposed to be private. To me, that's what it's always been. Sex has always been important but it's never been a deal breaker.

I've never even thought about taking the time to explore my sexuality. In the early days, I guess we would talk about sex sometimes. Now, it's—do you want to take a nap or go to bed? We've never played out any sexual fantasies.

When we first met, we used to spend all weekend in bed. Now if we're in bed, we're usually sleeping because we're tired. So age has made that difference for us. The only difference I can see is that the stamina we used to have is gone.

Actually, we're both pretty conservative when it comes to sex. He's of the same mind as I am. Then came the kids and we'd sneak it when we could, between their naps, so we would make time then. Now the kids have moved out and we have all the time in the world and we look at each other and go, huh? But it's a comfortable relationship. We don't have to prove ourselves to each other. I don't think anything's changed, except for the length, brevity, quantity.

I can see why the guys want to have the big Cialis and Viagra, where guys would want to have the same length of time they had when they were younger. To me it's ridiculous. We're just not the same as we were when we were younger.

**✳✳✳**

I like about sex that it's relaxing. It reduces stress. Every once in a while you just feel like you need it. I can't think of anything I don't like.

I am very conservative about this and kind of uncomfortable talking about what I will and won't do sexually. At the same time, I step back and find it all very funny. I laugh a lot about other people's sex.

Actually, everything my husband does must be endearing because I've stuck with him for so long … I must enjoy it. I think we've kind of grown up with one another. We know what each other likes, so that makes it easier.

If you want to talk about what's annoying, I could give you tons of advice. Foreplay is very important for a woman and having someone who's willing to do that is the key. You can't cock us like a gun, we don't work like that. To have someone who's willing to go the extra mile for you, that's very important. And that's something he does for me. The thought of him just doing me then rolling over and going to sleep, leaving me there, that isn't going to work.

I didn't count on sex as my top priority. When we first started going out, I looked for a good personality, someone who made me laugh and had a good sense of humor, someone who was kind and thoughtful—maybe not always to me, but good daddy material, educated. These were the things I thought outweighed sex.

So I guess what I'm saying is that if every other thing was excellent and the sex was so-so, I probably would be very attracted to a man. If the sex was great and he, as a person, sucked I probably wouldn't have married. I think there are very many more important things that a woman needs to look for—like someone who could be your best friend, watching your back rather than you on your back.

I think there's a level of trust that's important. There were lots of other things I was looking for besides sexual prowess—if sex went away tomorrow, I don't think it would change us because there are much more important things that bind us together.

I would suggest women become friends before they became lovers. Or you can do it simultaneously, but I would make sure he's a good friend.

Friends and friendship are more important than anything else. Respect—that goes with friendship too. I would never intentionally hurt a friend. I would never intentionally hurt your feelings. So all those things women have as friendship, I expect that and more from a guy, then sex is just thrown in as an extra added benefit.

\*\*\*

My husband knew all about foreplay and taking his time. He likes boobies so that helps in the foreplay. He was also married before, so maybe someone else had trained him before he got to me. There's also eight years difference between us. I think it takes guys at least four or five years to catch up to women, so he was three or four years ahead of me sexually—ha, ha!

I just like him—that was most important to me—everything else pretty much worked out for the last thirty-two years. Since I had a hysterectomy when I was thirty-two years old, I really haven't had a menopause per se or any change in my sex drive from that.

\*\*\*

Today, how would I define a good girl? I'd like to think my daughters are good girls, but I don't want to judge. I don't think it should even be an issue for anyone under the age of sixteen. Like my parents wouldn't let me date anybody until I was sixteen … and then I didn't anyhow. For anybody younger than that, running around with the wrong crowd and/or dressing provocatively, could get you in trouble. I told my daughters, 'I know you are you, but people do judge you, so you really need to dress appropriately.'

What is a good girl? Someone who gets their shit together, finishes school, is able to support herself, because it's no longer a world of one income. The girl should be equal to the guy in all of those respects. And a good girl could be good but people may make her sound bad, so a good girl is someone who has a high self-esteem, knows what she wants.

Actually, I don't know what's a good girl or a bad girl. One of my daughters dresses crazy and yet she's a lawyer and I know she's always been a good girl. It's hard to explain what a good girl is. Does is really have anything to do with your sexuality?

I'm not particularly proud of myself, of what I did when I was twenty. My mom was married and had kids by twenty. It's an age appropriate question, I think, about what's good or bad.

At the same time, when you're twenty and you sleep around, well, you're twenty and you sleep around. So what? If you're twelve and sleep around, or sixteen, I think you should get the lay of the land first.

It's not a good girl/bad girl issue—it's a growing up issue. Kids should be educated about sex and diseases and relationships. In grammar school or junior high, then it's a good girl/bad girl issue. Seventeen, eighteen, nineteen—I don't have a problem with someone sleeping with someone then. I don't see it as a problem, as much of a prude as I am.

There were times when I had two boyfriends in a day ... but since I did it myself, I didn't feel like a bad girl. And I don't regret it. I guess maybe I was wild at twenty, but I'm not a bad girl really. It's hard to label things good or bad because it makes such a judgment on other people ... or yourself.

\*\*\*

I think my girlfriends had more to do with how I grew up than religion. The people you hang out with are very important. The girls I hung out with were just like me—we played sports and other things. Sex wasn't even in our awareness.

On the other hand, there is guilt. The church is built on guilt. It did affect me but only as an afterthought. I think who you hang out with is still more important. I was always very straight arrow and a very good girl until I was nineteen or twenty, then I went to college. I was twenty-four when I met my husband. My mother and father would just shake their heads at me during that time.

I did date a lot but I didn't necessarily go to bed with all of them. The other things—laughter, acceptance, friendship—were way more important to me. My daughters are like me.

When I look back, I'm not sure the 70s did us any favors. Women still aren't equal. We don't get paid the same. I expect equality across the board. Actually, women have to work harder now to get anywhere than when I was growing up. It started in the 80s. It requires two incomes to live now and that was just twenty-five years ago.

.So maybe we became equal sexually, but maybe it only looked like sexual equality but wasn't really.

\*\*\*

These are my words of wisdom for all our daughters and granddaughters. I would make sure I was friends with him first, before sex. I would make sure we're friends first—that you get along, that he gets you, that you get him, that he has a sense of humor. Friendship is very hard to break, where marriages seem very easy to break.

To me sexy is someone who is nice ... just like me ... only a guy. Considerate and kind.

Be a friend and then be a lover. Those were my words to my daughters. Have friends, hang out with them. Forever is a long time. Can you stand to hang out with him? If you don't even like him as a person—the way he laughs, the way he demeans people—if you don't like that now, it's not going to get any better. The early days are when the guys are on their best behavior!

Understand each other and be friends. I have friends that go back from when I was six years old. We went to grammar school together and we still talk. Friendships last. Those are the only words of wisdom from me today.

I'm of the belief that you always treat people the way you want to be treated, so if you want to call someone a bad girl, do you really want someone calling you a bad girl? There's a lot of girls out there, we all come from different economic situations ... some parents are educated ... some are single.

Who am I to judge? The woman who ran for vice president—Palin—her daughter was seventeen and pregnant. Was she a good girl or a bad girl? She was definitely uninformed, she claims. One mistake does not make someone good or bad.

# 13

# Elizabeth

I wrote a book about all my sexual adventures with George as a partner. He was my first husband. You should see pictures of us, I was so swollen with hormones, I lactated. I was 47 yrs old and a nut! Now I'm finally into a passionate, exciting, intellectually and sexually satisfying relationship. My oldest son just said to Warren on Sunday, 'I'm so glad my mom has you. You're the only person in the whole world who is able to deal with her.'

We're living in a society that doesn't value women's sexuality or women ourselves. We're very powerful. It's a real put down being a sexual woman. We grew up when we were told that good girls not only don't do it, but good girls don't like doing it.

If we talk to each other about our sexuality and the sexual journey we've taken over the last thirty to forty years—what's changed, what's ended up being important—and then we put it out there, maybe our daughters and granddaughter will have an easier time.

Maybe we can put the end to this myth—more of a bad controlling story—about women's sexuality. Women have always been sexual—read *The Chalice and the Blade*. We make human life out of our own bodies—how sexual can you get?

This myth of good girl/bad girl was absolutely part of the high points of my growing up. The construct was the Presbyterian church. That was extremely controlling for me and all the girls were told, 'You should save yourself for marriage and basically don't have fun being a person.' My family was very involved in the church. I could see it in the neighborhood, too, filled with Catholics and others. I never knew a Black or a Jew. I was raised in Seattle.

The whole neighborhood was made up of church people of one sort or another. That was the controlling influence, because even if you were going to disobey your parents, you wouldn't want to disobey God. So the parents were using the power of the church to suppress and control, particularly girls. The boys seemed to be having a different story forming—'whatever you could get.'

I found myself just absolutely being needy and falling in love with guys at church camp when I was fourteen. I was accused by an older friend of being starved for affection. I was a battered child. My parents fought constantly. My mother was a Catholic who changed to Presbyterian for my father. My father was a steward of the church. I thought he maybe would be involved, but it was mostly my mom who stayed active in the church.

There we were at these church camps that were hotbeds for hormonal kids … running around in the middle of the night and doing everything else. I come to find out that, because of my personality type, I am more sexual, like Clinton is. There's a parallel with the charisma and passion and the feelings, except I liked sex more than my sisters do, who are colder and more rigid. My birthday is July 2 and I have a Cancer sun and moon with a Sagittarian rising.

*\*\*\**

In tenth grade, there was a guy who was really sexy to me and I'm just not going there with him. He was being coached by one of the guys at his father's used car lot, and he could drive all these new little cars around. There was also a trailer. So he was trying to get me into that trailer. It's been so long since I thought about this. Basically all it took was just one workout, then I couldn't stay away from sex.

But he was an awful person. He wasn't a good person and he didn't love me … but I was instantly addicted to the sex. I was fifteen. I thought that was it. I remember when we spent the next summer at church camp, we were supposed to throw faggots into the fire to represent our sin. And I couldn't find anyone in the Bible who fit my situation, so I said my sin was adultery. That seemed to be the closest thing. There wasn't anything in the Ten Commandments that spoke to my sin.

Especially since we carried on doing it. Then I thought I was pregnant. I was fifteen, I'd only had sex for three months, and then I hadn't started my period. I went to the minister. 'You shouldn't be doing this,'—'Oh no, I'm swearing off.' Then he found out I was seeing the guy again. I figured he was going to call my mother. We had one phone that was tied into the line, so I had put a little glass to hold the thing up off the receiver.

Then this asshole minister tells his wife, who told other people in the church, who made my life really hard. Around New Years I started my period, and I realized I didn't give a shit about God and I didn't want to go back to that church.

A bad girl wasn't a virgin anymore. That's what I was told, only to find out that there were all these people who were good girls who were doing it, and I didn't know it. That really bit. Then there was the next boyfriend who didn't love me either, but at least he had a little higher standard and nicer family.

It was always kinda dicey for me. I gave up the church before I gave up the sex. I felt so betrayed by the minister talking to his wife about me. I think that I was able to discern quite early on that there was a difference between the church and God.

***

I got married at nineteen at the same church. I was still working on feeling better and being better about myself. Here comes the sexual thing again, though. For me, having a child meant that I could right the wrong of my previous behavior.

That a healthy baby, a beautiful child came out of that same place—it was very primitive, very superstitious, in that having the baby would somehow make *me* right. During my pregnancy, I thought I was going to have a kid with three heads because of the bad sexual stuff I thought I had done. I wanted to be sure, but they didn't have ultrasound. I was so huge they thought I was going to have twins. So they x-rayed me—then I worried the kid was going to have leukemia.

During that pregnancy, I was just a mess because I figured I wasn't under the canopy of God's goodness and blessings because of all the bad teachings of the church.

It was the sex outside of marriage that had made me a bad person. And because I was the bad seed—that's why I had been abused. I remember my father beat me up once in the front yard. I was like hamburger. I thought he was the jerk then—I was six years old—but you can't stay with that in your mind all the time. My mother was always saying, 'If you just keep your mouth shut, he wouldn't do that.' But I was never able to keep my mouth shut and I enraged him again and again. So I got married to escape that.

I met my husband on my way to university. After two quarters at school, he talked me into getting married. I quit school to go to work so I could afford a real trousseau. He was from a wealthy family with lots of stuff, Hawaiian vacations, gorgeous rings. My thought was, 'Now my dad can't hit me anymore.'

When I was six months pregnant, we were invited to hear an Episcopal priest at a pot-luck dinner for young people. I said 'God is just a crutch.' He said, 'Why don't you need one?' There were people being healed, speaking in tongues, laying in the Spirit—people were experiencing all these amazing miracles.

I always thought the problem with the church was that Jesus was all so distant. It was mostly all about rules. So along comes a really intelligent, dynamic, charismatic priest who had three kids. So we went every Saturday evening to this group. And more and more I was just listening. Finally we went down to the church. It was like a rally or gospel thing and somebody stood up and witnessed, saying the sins of the father will be visited upon the sons for every generation.

It was like everybody's dad was feared—it seared my heart open. I felt like God was calling me. I waited until after the baby was born, because I wouldn't give my heart to a god that would give me a deformed kid. The priest came to the hospital to see me. He prayed with me, talked about how I'd been blessed.

A month later we went down to the church to another one of those meetings. We were all invited to go into the church and kneel at the altar and have laying on of hands and participate in the Holy Spirit—speaking in tongues with somebody interpreting. The music was Abba, for heaven sakes! Ha ha!

This was so astonishing. I have never ever not believed, from that point on. I was just filled with electric joy … an absolutely astonishing new beginning in our lives. We were really drawing everything to us.

Then we got really pious and it changed us, including the sex. The sex was great, it always was. He was gentle and he knew what to do. I had internal orgasms. It was magical to me, especially having the whole baby thing and then the god thing. It was just ecstatic.

As soon as we got married, I had begun to feel like a good girl—because sex was sanctioned and because he was a good man and the opposite of my father. I felt I'd made a good choice. I still wasn't into the whole evolved God thing yet, but at least I'd done the right thing by my church, playing by the rules.

The question is deeper than that, though. How did I feel during sex? I was in a marriage where I didn't have to worry about money and I was grateful. It's really interesting because I think there's always some kind of embarrassment in sex. I felt in some ways that God was outside the bedroom because it was still personal.

Like blowjobs, for instance. There was stuff floating around about how good girls didn't do that. We women didn't used to share everything with each other—that came later. At the same time, sometimes I'd say 'Hail Mary, full of grace, help me come better.'

I was a screamer and that created a problem. We moved to a place that had a skylight that opened. The landlord called to say the neighbors were complaining to the police that someone was being murdered. I finally got away from my dad and then I start screaming—way over the top!

Some things naturally transitioned within the marriage, which was proper. But it got nasty sometimes, like dildos, sticking things up my ass and his ass. We needed the extra things to turn us on because there wasn't any intimacy to connect us up on the intellectual and emotional level.

It got weird. My daughter just told me the same thing about her marriage … the sex got weird when the marriage started to go bad. We were married twenty-four years. To leave that was very difficult.

\*\*\*

I wrote two chapters of my novel before I left the marriage. I was essentially writing myself out of the marriage. I was always about three months behind in terms of what was happening in my life and what I was recording.

What I found in the writing was that I was moving into this space where I was comparing the sex act with the communion. I laughed once realizing that over the duvet cover I had put a lace tablecloth. It wouldn't be used for anything. How weird is that? It was like an alter cloth, in a way, in the middle of my bed.

With my first husband, there was all this 'no touching me while I was on my period.' Warren, my second husband, didn't care. We did it anywhere, anytime. He was just so natural about it. Warren kept asking about what my first husband and I had thought about shitting and peeing and menstruating. It's all natural, Warren would say!

He was my ground. I remember being in that cozy comfy bed with the tablecloth saying, 'Take me, this is my body.' Saying that it was the communion, that my vagina was the chalice. I just loved it all. Oooh, oooh, oooh.

I'm an artist, a poet in my life. The sex, the cello, the food, church, house, sitting, the rugs, the pillows, the children, the grandparents, hair styles, everything just seemed all God. The basic deliciousness of everything. I'd be weeping in grocery stores at the colors.

It seemed to me that this is the way you should be as an artist. I'm constantly turned on by everything now.

I was talking to a friend with problems—something like, he doesn't want her to touch him and they've been married for thirty-two years and he has something on the side. They never have sex and they sleep at opposite ends of the house. I said I've never been without sex for more than two weeks in my life—since I've been fifteen years old. Some of that was self-pleasuring.

That's the other thing—about masturbation. It's all God. It's all thank you. It's all being grateful. Imagine being able to feel that good. You'd have to be an idiot to not understand that it's there, not just to procreate. It's there. It's such ecstasy.

I think my sexing could be like a lot of peoples' but it doesn't have to be, if you draw it out. To be sexually active in my sixties is pretty special to me.

We women can still be interested and capable, after menopause. And we deliberately evolved that way for some reason.

I see my friends who have quit their jobs, they're retired. They drink more, their backs hurt. They've lifted toilets or pounded nails too hard, too much impact stuff. There's not that juice anymore—they are withering up.

We went to dinner with a couple the other night. I said to my husband later, 'Don't they seem so old?' They started buying senior tickets ten years ago. They seem that much older. You gotta have some faith to stay young.

I think sex is energy you need to move through your body. It lubricates everything, including the brain. If a woman doesn't have sex after menopause, she becomes a dried up old hag—dried up versus juicy and alive. It's the sex that keeps the juices flowing. It's a hormonal thing. Who knows what sponsors what, it's probably a Mobius strip. That's why I told my husband he had to quit his job that had him up three nights a week auditing a hotel.

Everything started to go away during that time. He had problems staying awake. He wasn't interested in sex either. We went a whole month with that. I told him I was scared by it. We weren't old but we were acting like it. I've done the math, you take six of your relatives, take out the one who died the youngest, then divide the rest by five and you know how old you can get. For me it's ninety-six. Even my dad, who's had a terrible stroke and been dragging his body around for eighteen years, he's eighty-nine.

\*\*\*

I was very monogamous in my first marriage, but also very attracted to people. The more he traveled, the more stress there was on the marriage. He was always home on the weekends and there was always sex. But it got embarrassing because there wasn't an emotional connection. I was mad at him for going away. He was mad at me for spending money. 'I'm earning a living!' he'd yell, 'doing government contracts, top security, good money, pentagon jobs back east.'

If we went on vacation … the first time we went to Europe we did it every night. 'Fuck me in France' 'I'm making love in Paris!' It was magical lavender misty Paris to me—everything was a turn on—the food, the sights and sounds. It was 1984, my fortieth birthday. We went first class for three weeks and we spent $13,500. Everything was a five star hotel. It was fabulous. I bought clothes and other stuff along the way. There weren't any children with us. It was pretty great … and the bidets!

\*\*\*

I'd gone back to school and I was attracted to everybody. I was in the playwriting class, all this drama, looking right in people's eyes. Really exciting.

Somebody said recently I practice Socratic seduction. What's that? There's all this logic but it's so seductive. That's why people give me money. 'She can do it,' they believe about me.

There I am, turning people on, being turned on, but not wanting to go against the church or God. I really thought I could leave the church out of it, since I know what God wants from me and it's not to be unfaithful in a marriage. I got really attracted to this one guy, a professor, who was also a member of our church.

We went out to lunch one day, sitting in a Holiday Inn bar—we were the only people in there. And the glass was getting more and more covered with fingerprints. He had this serious thing going on. We were kissing. When I got home I think I had to masturbate every 10 minutes.

I told my husband, 'We gotta do something because I don't know what to do any more.' He said 'Oh God.' Then I was staging things so I would meet the guy, even when I was with my husband.

The professor said he was going to a play, to support a colleague. I went out to the play, about the children's crusade. The guy I was flirting with wasn't there. But I introduced myself to the playwright. He said he'd read my poetry. I was ready to sail off into the wild blue yonder with him. He said, 'I'd love to have you in a class.' So that began my career ...

My first play won two awards. It was about sex with the professor. All the god stuff was in there, with the bad girl stuff, the 'what do you do in this kind of a situation' stuff, and the 'how to make the marriage work' stuff. It was a very difficult play to resolve. It was essentially the gestalt of what I was living through, going to therapy.

We put a mom and dad on stage, with him saying he was going to hit her with the gold club card. Everything was related to an amusement park, a playland. I just wanted to be in the tunnel of love, I didn't want to be in the haunted house.

Around this time I had the dream about being in the depression house with my hands scotch taped to the wall, realizing I could leave if I just pulled it off. All these people saw me pull my arms away from the flimsy scotch tape, I had figured it out. I ran out and they all followed me. I ran out to the cliff. I was about to dive in the water and they said 'You don't even know how to swim.' I dove anyway. I went down down down under the water. As I was coming up, I saw webbed feet, and when I came up it was a swan. I got on the back of the swan and that's when I woke up. I figured I was lost. The swan is a symbol of monogamy. About that time I was debating whether to have an affair or not.

I opened the Bible and flipped the pages, then pointed. It said, 'How long will you hesitate to foil the other, for God is making something new upon the earth. The woman sets out to find her husband again. Mark the way by which you came.'

I interpreted that to mean I was going to find 'him,' I was going to spend all of my passion and energy to find 'him' again. I didn't want to lose 'him.' I loved 'him.' I didn't know what that meant exactly—resurrecting the dead, or just being kinder. I tried everything. As you can well imagine, I can be pretty demanding. I just kept getting more and more unhappy.

I was having some success professionally. I was hired to write on a tv show, and then I had some of my own money. It was getting fun for me—the children were a little older—I was winning prizes. At the same time, at home, the more I unhappy I got, the more looking around I did. I didn't know how to be without a man. I didn't, but I didn't really want Warren either, the new man I'd just met.

The first thing I thought was I'd never take his last name. We became friends. I was lonely even though I hadn't separated from my husband yet. I was a single wife, all week long. One of the kids was gone—the oldest told me I had a fucked marriage, the littlest one was eleven and unhappy because daddy didn't do anything with him. I had a lot of time on my hands. I started writing this novel.

Warren would go out with me because he was lonely too ... he'd been out of a marriage for about a year, living alone with another guy roommate. We would just have fun, go bowling, riding bikes—he was interesting and he was interested in me. There was a real attraction ... but not really.

He came to lunch. I asked him to take my boots off. I was wearing bright red lipstick and I just kissed him. His tongue went into my mouth and I thought oh no, then we had a kiss that was a mad thing. It was pretty soon after that he came over in the evening when George, my husband, was gone and I said, 'I really want you to make love to me.' He said, 'I'm not going to be used like that.' I said, 'Just fuck me, I would feel better, then you can go away.' He said, 'No, that's not the way it works. Then we'd be involved and you're not free.' Then I said, 'I hate you, go away,' and slammed the door. He came the next day and I slammed it again.

It was a month later that George and I went to Palm Desert to be with our friends, one of whom was the CEO of Northrop. We went to a tennis match and we stayed at their posh little condo. On the way over, George was late so we ended up in horrible traffic. I berated him for being late and stupid about traffic. He just kept taking it and taking it. I ragged on him all over dinner. I finally figured out, it's bad enough I abuse him, but that he lets me abuse him? I couldn't imagine being in that marriage anymore. I was so upset and disappointed, it was so over. I made a decision for no love making with him ever again. I didn't want to be in that marriage.

After the weekend, when he left on Monday morning to fly back east, I lay in bed and said 'I divorce you,' three times. I'm done. I called Warren, 'I'm getting a divorce. He doesn't know it yet but he's probably figured it out.'

I said, 'Can I come take you to dinner?' On the way I bought him a shirt and tie, put it on the charge account. It became a very romantic sexual relationship. It was different because there had been so much pressure and build up that Warren was just hard all the time and there was no problem. George had been different. Warren was just this rod that could perform all the time.

There were still overtones of good and bad at that point. I felt I was divorced because I had said it three times. I knew there would be formality still to do, so we went to the priest, Warren and I. We said, 'We're not going to make this public in the church but somebody saw us last week and we want you to know what's going on.' The priest said, 'You know there's such a thing as adultery and there are warnings to keep you from falling into the pit.' I said I had already been in the pit and I'm not now.

At one point my ex called the priest and said, 'Well, you know she's living in sin?' I had moved out and I was getting a divorce immediately.

Then Warren and I weren't getting along, and then we were, and then we weren't. The first thing that happened when I moved in was, he bought a whole big bag of marijuana and stayed high the whole time. He's an alcoholic, hadn't had a drink in two years, but... it was like he was terrified—can it work with her?

It was too much pressure for him, he didn't handle it well at the time. He turned into a raving asshole and I had to kick his ass, back and forth. Finally I said, 'You've just got to go to AA,' and I went to Alanon. We were doing tons of therapy.

At the time, the priest told me my ex said 'You're living in sin.' I said 'No I'm not, I'm living in a cute little house on the Riviera. Get over it.' 'You're not married and you're living with him.' I said, 'Shoot me.'

I wasn't acting out good girl/bad girl anymore. There was a realization that that sex stuff was good, I was more alive, kinder, happier. I was with somebody that was my equal. I was having profound erotic and religious experiences—it was all one thing to me. I was over the bad girl stuff but there were still hard things I had to deal with.

I went over and saw the aging bishop and told him my whole story. And he said, 'Great. God loves you. What's your problem? And it sounds like Warren loves you too.'

I was writing this book so I was articulating everything. The past was being worked out in my writing, and I was able to see what that all meant, instead of swimming around in it.

Then there was the Alanon meetings ... where everybody was a battered child, so I wasn't that special anymore either. People actually do get on with it ... that finally dawned on me!

There was the love addiction where I couldn't stand it if Warren wouldn't tell me we were going to make love that night. We got real co-dependent for awhile. So we went to co-dependent Alanon. We just availed ourselves of everything.

\*\*\*

The bad girl would come up when I would doubt whether I was on the right path—personally, not necessarily what society said. The superstitious thing came up too. What I've heard myself say is that if I feel good I think God is on my side. If I don't feel good or somebody says something that makes me doubt myself, then I don't feel like a good girl. I feel like somebody who did a bad thing and I'm going to have to pay for that.

But in my evolved state, I know that there is no such thing as crime and punishment in that sense. We are evolving creatures and I'm loved and blessed. It's up to me to decide what I will draw to myself, by my will.

Warren and I had this huge thing about a month ago. He's quit smoking and now he's not getting REM sleep. I bought a Mercedes one day while he was taking a nap and he got really pissed off. 'How are we going to pay for it and how are . . . ? Money money, money! I know you're going to get this money from your investors and where will that leave me?'

Sex and money! Hottest topics. Meanwhile he's making nothing, but killing himself doing it. He couldn't stop yelling at me and couldn't stop being angry. I said, 'Why don't you just leave and go away for awhile. I can't stand this anymore. Stay at the hotel.' That was a Tuesday. My daughter came up on Friday. She's leaving her husband and we're both laughing. By Monday he wanted to talk. But the whole time I was thinking, this is what happens when you indulge yourself in an adulterous relationship and it's not working out. It's punishment for being a bad girl. Since I was eighteen I've thought that about myself

\*\*\*

It's like the stigmata or something. It's there, it's branded, you can't get rid of it, maybe the scar moves up, but if you poke around in your hair you find it. It's never really gone, that weighing on of judgment, that thing that's only there to control you within a construct that society has deemed is the opposite of anarchy.

Because what I see is—with the right wing politicos and the strict father model and bullshit pope and the Mormon church—they are all afraid of us women. The men are all deeply afraid of us. Deeply ... because they can't figure us out.

The whole new thing about the y and x chromosome—the x is the male and we have the y, we're just that much more complicated than men are. Men are mostly the same—pretty predicable, but there are all different types of women.

The more power we get, the less power it seems we have. If we make power moves like a man, we're called manipulative. If we're clever, we work around the male ego in ways he can't see. Just as often, manipulation can come out in very unhealthy things, like grudge-bearing forever; backstabbing; the passive-aggressive kind of crap.

I feel like the more power I get, the kinder I am and the more generous I feel. It's not that there aren't women who get power and abuse it. That's because they haven't had it, or their mothers didn't have it; or they honestly have never had a decent role model of a powerful woman who is also kind and not neurotic, like all the ones on tv ...

However, like the woman columnist said, 'A man could write the columns I do and never be called a bitch or a bastard. They are just called strong.' I was told by a man the other night that I was a scourge. I said, 'Get over it. You just told me that your ideal life is to lie in bed and watch videos. I'm trying to get something done here. Am I ambitious, am I passionate, assertive, even aggressive? You bet I am. But we wouldn't be having this conversation about why I am this way, if we weren't in Santa Barbara.'

I'm totally one of the crowd in New York, and nobody in Europe thinks that I'm over the top. Even in LA people do things, so don't ...

***

Getting back to the whole thing about men, I don't think men feel very powerful. They're like children. From the moment they're a tiny bit socially aware, they're burdened with having to make a living, trying to figure out how to do that for the majority of their lives.

I watched my boys. It's like a burden. I've got one that's gonna make millions because he's so scared. And one that's living in abject poverty because he can't figure it out and he's dyslexic. He keeps going from one branch of the service to another.

Then I've got the artist kid who's wondering if she's ever going to be able to paint. She's pregnant, she's got to be the breadwinner, hence no time to paint.

I've only felt that since I've been cut loose from money and alimony stuff. It's really scary. We live in a merchant society. You're either a merchant or you're worthless, that's every message we get. What was the first message after 9/11? Go spend money! Can you imagine Roosevelt telling the people after Pearl Harbor. 'Go shopping!' We were down in San Diego recently. I cannot believe the shopping down there. Wednesday, Thursday, workdays, people driving into the mall, buying more crap than I've ever seen.

The chapter I'm in right now in terms of my life, is that I was given the opportunity to option a book to turn into a screenplay that is about sex and death. The main character is a woman who is an author and Russian opera singer. She's being treated by Sigmund Freud for a hysterical illness in her left ovary and left breast. There is no physical reason for her to feel this pain. She's been to every doctor. He's trying to figure out why she's feeling this way.

Meanwhile, she's having the most erotic sexual fantasies, like the soldier on the train breathing up her dress. With Freud, she doesn't tell him everything. He says, 'We can deal with this, but first we have to go back and understand where this comes from, why you're so upset … and hung up about sex.' It turns out that her mother and her uncle died in a hotel fire, because they were lovers.

Did the child know this but didn't know it? Freud thinks this is what it's all about, but he tells her to keep a journal. So she goes away to a spa in the mountains with her aunt and comes back with this erotic fantasy where there are breasts floating in the air and pounding amazing sex with his penis in her as she's walking up the stairs. Every time they make love, parts of the hotel either burn down or people are lost at sea or they fall out of windows. People are dying all around them. It's almost like the sex was produced—it sponsors the fire. Everybody mourns for a little while but then they go on with their lives. Like life.

But there's this incredible erotic awareness within this woman. She writes all this down into her journal. Then the dime finally drops. Freud thinks he's healed her, because the pain goes away. It turns out these are premonitions. She ends up outside of Kiev, where the holocaust began in Russia, and she jumps before she's shot, falling into the pit. A German comes along and stomps on her left breast and her left ovary.

This is the kind of mystery of life. She feels vile, and like a bad girl for having these extraordinary erotic fantasies. I totally identify with that. I also understand what a relief it is to live in that erotic, lovely, happy place (the little death). Freud, when he reads this journal, says sex and death are at war within this body, and sex is winning … because we have to choose between sex and life all the time—death meaning destruction, as opposed to moving on to the next level.

My theory evolved that the clit and a woman's capacity for these profound orgasmic sacred experiences—as the bridge to the transcendent—is not by accident. *And*, that makes women the bridge to the sacred. Our profound joyous sexual orgasmic ecstatic experiences are as close to God as we can get when we're in the body. There is no other experience as close as that. As a species, as we perturbate to the next level of consciousness, the energy, the fuel, the mechanisms that take us there are these profound orgasmic experiences.

When I've been making music I've occasionally thought, this is better than sex and I can die now. I've done it, I've seen it, I've felt that energy. And that never goes away. This is God, which is all along what Depok Chopra and *The Power of Now* guy say– they're all saying the same thing.

Now, though, we're living through the strict father model, with the man dictating.

We use words like—authentic, mystical and sacred. I don't often use those words, but it is what I'm describing. The sacred, if you turn those two letters around, it spells scared. You're either in the sacred or you're in fear, either scared or in this other place. It is about the inward being manifested outward.

***

There is a saying—the world is only one story away from transformation, whatever story that might be. In our worlds, the story we're reading now is the one transforming our world. The story that we're going to tell about all us women is transforming. I'm most drawn to theatre and film as the medium to tell these stories, because you only get to say three and a half things. You can only learn three issues at a time.

There's a way to do it. When you look at what people are so hungry for, not just women but men too. I saw men with a Mona Lisa smile—so what are women about anyway? But we need to do better at that, better at cinema. A friend says tv is better than it should be and film is worse than it should be. It's so hard to hook somebody, tell a story and make it compelling, all in two hours. It just takes craft. It was easier to write the libretto for an operetta than to write a screenplay. You have to write parts that represent a giant iceberg—the tip is the story, the underneath mass is the setting and society.

The actor's body does one part but the words have to imply this giant idea, using setting, socio-psychological stuff, everything. It's hard. If I'm not writing, I'm working a crossword puzzle because I love the puzzle, the challenge.

***

So, I've basically only been with two men in my life. No, there was this one guy, I think that was the only one. And, I've been monogamous with each of them ... except for that one time ...

I was crazy. I'd kicked Warren out. I ran into this person who I knew was a writer and I knew he wanted to know me. It turns out he was one of those roué types, never been married, fifty years old—really sad. Every woman I've ever known thought he was a catch ... until they knew he wasn't. What an asshole ... and a terrible way to waste time—his work, his whole life. You can't call it making love, what we did. We had this thing one night and then I went away to cello camp and I can't remember if we did it again. It was sad. There wasn't a connection.

I've counseled guys about this. I don't know very many women where the heart isn't connected to the sex organs. I don't get it when it isn't. I think it's sad and I think guys can somehow draw the line there, but I can't. I really have to be in love with somebody.

***

Today I do not believe there is such a thing as a bad girl. I like the C.S. Lewis definition—he called them brown girls. They're just about that far out of the dirt. They are women who aren't empowered, who don't get the fun or the eroticism or anything, it's just fucking to them. They may be temptresses—whatever you want to call them—but they are not connected to themselves.

Brown girls kinda reminds me of brownies or fairies, not fully human, not fully authentic, they are lesser beings somehow. Some women I've seen, even my age or only a little younger, are still out there trying to pick up men and devaluing themselves.

I don't like the words good and bad—even though I know we're using it here—because it's about applying a judgment to oneself or internalizing a judgment from society. On the spectrum of not fully evolved to totally evolved, those women C. S. Lewis called the brown girls do exist. Are they bad or are they just not fully alive? I've known them in various situations where they'd screw anybody. What's that about? Why are they so self-annihilating? Why are they not asking for more from life?

***

I don't feel bad, ever. I feel holy. Not to insult anybody, but here I am, I have this image of myself that is very goddess like, especially with these grown children and grandchildren, and one that is exactly like me, more than any of my children ever were.

I feel like all these amazing people came out of my body. And to have my third granddaughter say 'I came out of my mom's body and my mom came out of your body. Where did you come from?' 'Well, I came of out Gramma Millie's body.' 'Oh, no!' she said, so I showed her the Russian dolls.

***

I would love to leave a legacy for that granddaughter and all the other granddaughters out there—something she could learn at seventeen, instead of at fifty-seven.

I want you all to know that you are perfect. You can choose the best for yourself. You can have the most exciting, joyful fun in bed with somebody that you love. That's like beyond measure, isn't it? To comfort you and you to comfort someone else! To have … it would be hard for me to tell her this because it seems so intimate, but I can wish it and hope she can orchestrate it in a way what would be more subtle than this.

But my message is, I keep thinking of this book I read to my children—*You're Special*, You're the only one of your kind. God gave you a body and a fine perfect mind. It's such an instrument for creation of babies and music and food and loveliness and joy—and that's the bridge to the next existence.

To be fully alive in this one life so that you will recognize it in the next life. So that you won't be clinging to it because you will have already been there, because the sacred is everywhere. I would tell her there's nothing to be afraid of, ever. On some level she knows that.

I'd love to get any granddaughter a book on sex that didn't make it icky or too clinical. I think that's what novels and plays are about, and maybe really good movies. How do we get those to young people if they're about sex?

We had friends who would say to us, 'Are you really going to let your children see that movie?' Better than anything they could read in a book, it seemed to me. If they see people involved beautifully, lit right, making love like that, why wouldn't you want them to? It's attractive.

I had an aunt and uncle who were really caught up with each other and we all knew it. It was like being around a warm fire. It wasn't that they were displaying any bad behavior ... you just knew there was this sexual attraction. We knew they had a lot of fun in bed.

I wrote poems about them all the time. They were tall and very magical to me because life was so obviously fun for them.

I never mention to my granddaughters about having to get married, or 'Thou shalt not' or any of that stuff, because to me, that would flow out of the rest of her life—her having such joy in herself and life. She wouldn't be getting married for the wrong reasons. Already, she wants a baby so bad. She's wanted a baby for three years and she's just six now. She wrote it on the prayer wall as a wish—'I want a baby, I want to have a baby.' About that time, my other son adopted a little baby. Her response was, 'No, I want a baby out of my own body.' Where does that come from?

We celebrate that that's her wish. And that'll be great when it happens. It's like she gets to wear lip gloss when she goes to junior high. She gets to have babies when she grows up.

When she was twenty-two months old, she wanted to know about babies coming out of the pregnant mommy. There was the film about a pregnant bride. Now she wants to be a pregnant bride for Halloween. I tell you the books they are reading are really pretty impressive. And then there's pregnant Barbie. What's a grandmother to say?

# 14

# Akulina

The good girl/bad girl myth was definitely a part of my life, especially while I was living at home. Good girls don't do it. Bad girls do it. I probably first heard that in kindergarten—I was pretty advanced for my age. I understood sex, even then, because my parents always said sex was dirty, don't talk about it. It was clearly a taboo topic.

I didn't become sexually active until I was twenty-one, but it didn't have anything to do with the good girl/bad girl myth. It had to do with not being asked and not being interested in the right person. I didn't see any reason to just give it away for no reason. I was pretty unpopular, so I kinda did my own thing. I also didn't have any way to meet boys—I didn't belong to clubs or have much exposure after school.

My parents wanted me to study real hard. They were European and that's the way it was—you study hard and then get somewhere in life. I grew up in Holland.

If you just have sex for the fun of it, that was a bad thing. If you had sex because you loved somebody, that was okay. Although technically if you had sex outside of marriage that was still bad. I was born a Catholic and for us sex was a bad thing.

I broke with the Catholic Church and many myths disappeared along about the time I was thirteen. I remember the priest in Holland—he lived as poorly as the neighborhood, and he rode a bicycle. People put pennies in the poor box to support him.

Here in America, my very religious parents went to a church and were actually told not to come back because they didn't have the money to tithe the church. They were told they were not welcome. It was absolutely devastating to them. It totally turned me off to the church.

My early religious and spiritual teachings shaped my view of sex. Then I grew up and a lot of it changed—for me and my parents. I don't think it's about being a good girl/bad girl. I think, like everything else, sex is about making choices. There are consequences. If there's any good/bad about it, it's dealing with the consequences and being prepared . . . if possible.

I personally feel it's just another function of living. I find it interesting in this country, because everybody is so two-faced. On the one hand, you don't talk about it, and maybe you don't do it. On the other hand, everything is sold through sex. Every advertisement is about sex. Every commentary is about sex. In Europe, you get more of a feeling that sex is just one of the functions of being alive, whereas here, there is such a focus on it.

Even what people do in their bedrooms has such a focus on it. It's nobody's business, but it has become this huge big thing. Sex is only one aspect of living—it's not the most or the least important, it's one of a number of issues. Hunger, safety, money—things like that.

Then you see those preachers. Be careful of them, the more they preach, the more there's quite the skeleton in the closet . . . usually.

\*\*\*

I did long term relationships instead of marrying. In one period, I had several relationships—usually I'm pretty monogamous but in college I had several lovers at the same time. Everybody did at that time. What did I learn from it? Women are much more emotionally attached to sex than men are. For men, it's more of a physical thing.

I remember once having an argument with a guy who wanted to have sex right afterwards. No woman would want to do that. But to the guy, it's the way to make up. Men and women look at sex very differently and react to it very differently.

I explored my own sexuality a lot in my teenage years. Then in my twenties and thirties, my sense of myself as a sexual being really grew because that was when people were very stimulating and interesting and into exploration. Lovers didn't tell me what to do. They always suggested and asked. That's a very big aphrodisiac to me because I don't like people who tell me what to do, especially men.

\*\*\*

Now, my sex drive is pretty much turned off, that whole sexual part of me. It's been that way for awhile, primarily because a long term (ten year) relationship ended, and then I went through menopause, and then I started taking medication, which also decreased the sex drive. At this point, it's okay. There was a time when it would have been devastating if that had happened, but now it's okay.

I'm not even sure it's ended. I remember, maybe ten years ago, wondering 'Oh my god, what if this is the last time I ever have sex?' I don't think of it like that now, but the chances of my meeting another man and starting another relationship are slim. You never know. I wouldn't be totally against it, but I'm not going out bar crawling for it either.

My most active sex life still was pretty intermittent. My main love relationship was out of state. We'd have sex when we got together and traveled and that sort of thing.

I never considered myself a bad girl because I had sex and didn't get married. A bad girl would have been having unrelated sex. What I would consider a bad girl would be if you had HIV and didn't tell anybody when you passed it around. That would make you bad and the situation tragic. Things like abortions could be considered bad, some of them, but I believe in the right to abortion. That's about it in terms of bad.

I think sexuality is between two people and it's their own business. Obviously things like pedophilia are bad. Basically anything that's against someone's will, or something that's done to people who can't make decisions for themselves, like children, that's bad. But as far as expressing sex, I don't have any hang-ups about it having to be in marriage or whatever. I don't even have any hangups about it having to be with one person. Although I think if I was in one relationship I would like it to be monogamous, for a number of reasons, including health.

Why do they shove the good girl/bad girl paradigm down women's throats, when men don't get defined by it? It makes no sense, except to control her ... us. I hate that contradiction—the guy wants to marry the good girl but in the meantime he's deflowering every girl he can get. It's bullshit.

I think also a lot of it is from the churches, which are primarily male controlled. A lot of those obsolete decisions come because all churches are male oriented. If they were female oriented, maybe there would be interesting comments about what men do ... but you never hear about that.

Why can a man be sexual and it's okay, but women can't, even today?

Control, pure control—I believe—in the sense that the guys can do what they want, at the same time they want to make sure they can control the women. If they have a woman who is monogamous, they know who the kids belong to. And they don't have anybody else that the woman can compare them to. She might say, he's a better lover than you—and it becomes an ego performance issue for him.

\*\*\*

That is a special step—if the woman is monogamous and doesn't have sex with anybody else, then sex can actually bring you closer. If you care for somebody, sex is a nice way of expressing that.

I think women could be just as loose, playing the field. Just because women tend to be more emotional, it isn't the same as being monogamous at all. Women have just as much willingness to go with different partners, and we have just as much sex drive as men do.

I think men are very much afraid of women's sex drive. Why else are women's clitoris's cut off in Africa? Why are women's bodies covered? This has nothing to do with the women, this has to do with the men being able to control themselves ... or not wanting to have to control themselves! So all the burden and guilt is placed on the woman and you see it over and over in all kinds of cultures.

I think men can control women because they created and perpetuated the big old boy's club. They've been allowed to get away with it. One of the reasons I like the idea of women becoming empowered in the government and decision-making, is because until that happens this institutionalized sexism will continue.

Nobody is going to give up power if they don't have to. So it necessarily becomes a man versus a woman—the one who's got control and power versus the one who doesn't. I can't think of anybody who willingly wants to give up control or power. And that's a lot what it's about, I think.

Many women have willingly given up control over their own bodies and given over their power to men—voluntarily—that's very true. But I do see somewhat of a change. Go back to the 18$^{th}$ and 19$^{th}$ centuries, when marriage was a necessity because women weren't allowed to do anything by themselves, by law. That's what a woman did—she got married and if she was lucky, she used her beauty and sexuality to get someone who would feed her and support her and protect her.

Then, with the world wars, women had to take on war related duties and got a taste of what it was like to have a little freedom. They didn't particularly want to go back to being the little housewifey thing, when they could earn their own money and have some freedom. I think it scared the living daylights out of the guys. When men are scared, they make like it's the woman's fault.

I look at today. Guys very seldom want women that talk back to them. A good woman is one who is quiet, who does what she is asked to do and does it with a smile. A bad woman is one who questions, who has her own opinion and who isn't going to lay down because somebody says lay down. It happens day in and day out. It happens at work every day, where basically men still dominate women. They get upset with a woman who isn't easily dominated, in a way they wouldn't if it was a man doing it to them.

It comes from Christian roots. First of all, we have this whole thing with little myths that are supposedly the word of God. But they were written hundreds of years after the event. Most people can't even remember yesterday. So we're supposed to take verbatim, words that strangers have written about strangers? To me that makes no sense.

The same thing with the Adam and Eve myth. It's like, yeah, the woman was seen as the evil one, while the poor guy, what was he doing? Or the woman was made of Adam's rib and somehow that means she is inferior? I find it interesting that men are stronger physically than women. What would have happened if women had been physically stronger than men? What would that have changed?

That has a lot to do with initially why somebody got power. They certainly didn't do it through their brains. Rush Limbo saying things like, 'As long as I slew the saber tooth tiger for you, for years, you now have to do what I tell you to do. Sure, you risk your life having the babies, but you still have to do what I tell you.' The idea that because he's stronger, he has the right to dominate in all areas—it's ridiculous.

Now that some women are starting to enter politics, it will be interesting to see if, when women are 50% of the politicians, it will change the way politics are being played.

As so many women have entered the workplace and politics, they've become junior men. They're the frontrunners, but they have made so many compromises that they don't really represent feminine energy much anymore. It's like in the 80s when we went to work and we started wearing suits and ties. Junior men.

The funny thing is that in order to get there, you have to mimic their guy behavior, but then you get knocked down because you're not feminine enough. And yet any group that has had to fight for something, whether females or blacks, you have to mimic the status quo. It seems to me that initially you've got to be really extreme in order to break down barriers. Later on you can be more mainstream in your outlook. You never get anything by sitting quietly and saying thank you. You only get there with extremist behavior—it could be nonviolent but still extreme.

***

I don't like what I see happening—children having sex. I don't consider them old enough to have sex. I think people should wait up to a certain time, whether it's seventeen or eighteen or sixteen, whatever. If you don't have a well-developed sense of self and who you are, sex can easily drag you down. Just like dating someone, learning to be in a relationship is difficult and I think you need to be somewhat socially aware of what's happening before you can be successful at it.

I think sex can be a very positive thing ... well, it has positive and negative aspects. A person should be made very much aware of both, and how it can be used for good and bad. When it's used for control, it's negative.

Positively, from a health standpoint, it makes your little body run better. I think it's also a very positive expression of being close to someone and caring for someone, tightening the experience of closeness.

The main negative thing is that you can be used, really used through sex. For example, young girls sometimes will go and have sex because they want to feel close. And then, instead, they end up feeling thrown away. That can be very devastating to a young girl.

Later in life, can you still be used? At fifty, or older? For sure ... and in the same way. I think what happens a lot is, people confuse sex and love. Just like in relationships, women can still be used by guys who promise them all kinds of things. Women might see sex as a way to get hold of somebody or keep him or get him to like her better. Then she finds out she was just a play toy for the guy.

I think women do tend to equate sex with stronger emotions than men. Men can equate sex with very strong feelings of love, but they can also just be physical and it doesn't matter who she is. I think a woman can use a man sexually too. Definitely. I've seen it. It's the same thing as the person who drops her boyfriend. It's December and they don't want to be alone for the holidays so they take on a boyfriend and then drop him in the spring. How unfair is that?

\*\*\*

As far as annoying goes, cleanliness is my issue, or rather lack of cleanliness. The guy has to smell right to me. I'm not talking perfume, I'm talking the pheromones. My boyfriends always smelled good to me. There were men who were wonderful but they didn't smell right.

Cleanliness is part of that. Clean undies. None of this three day old he-man type stuff. It doesn't work for me. I don't like that unwashed smell, not me.

I can't describe what I do like. It's clean but it's not even a smell, in the sense that it's roses or soap or anything else. Some people have the smell I'm compatible with, and some don't.

I don't like the smell of a recently washed soapy body, because it doesn't have a natural smell. The smell of soap doesn't turn me on ... actually it turns me way off. I like a body that's maybe four to six hours out from a shower— that's when the natural body smells come.

It actually is a natural smell because, even when those guys sweat, it doesn't turn me off. But for other people, it's like the sweat smell is horrible! Even on a scientific scale, we're all different.

So, wrong smell is high on my list of annoying. Then there's 'wham bam, thank you ma'am.' I want foreplay, cuddling afterward, all of that. That's important. How very feminine of me. I think of my last lover, who didn't get it ... which is why he isn't a lover anymore.

The funny thing about making love ... it's one of those things that doesn't have anything to do with a textbook telling you, here's how you do it. It's all got to do with the physical act. It can be described very specifically but there is a whole range from this end to that end on how that one physical act can be done.

If you have a lover who is focused on pleasing you and going for what you need, and you do the same for that person, then it can be a really wonderful experience. I've been lucky to have lovers who took the time and did the extra things for me and who really enjoyed sex. I should say, who enjoyed making love. There's a difference. They enjoyed the rubbing and all the other stuff. That's what's great.

Sex has been satisfying for me but I haven't been orgasmic during sex. I never have been. I don't know why. When I masturbate, I orgasm. I would like to orgasm when I'm making love. I used to think, 'Oh my god, am I the only one who doesn't?' but then I talked to some friends of mine and found out it's quite common. The point is, if I enjoy it and he enjoys it, what difference does it make?

When I used to try to go for that end goal, the big O, I wasn't enjoying it anymore because I was so busy trying to get there. A very male thing— destination in sex. Men are designed for the outward ejaculation, and ejaculation is always an end goal. Unfortunately when you get there, all action stops. Not yet, not yet, I say!

I've never spent time taking classes or gotten help about the question of why I can orgasm by myself and not with another person. It hasn't really bothered me that much. I suppose if I was married, and it was causing a problem, then I probably would.

Oh, yeah, I've always been honest with the guys—I haven't faked it ... but only if they ask. I don't sit there and say, oh by the way I faked it ... because I don't think it was anything that they did. Maybe there wasn't enough trust there, on my side. Could very well be. I don't have very high trust when it comes to men. That's very common also.

**\*\*\***

Guys can be endearing. I was in the shower one time and I come out of the shower and there's this perfectly made cup of coffee, just the way I love it, standing there. It was great. I connected that with sex. I like men to be feminine at times in the sense of doing things like that cup of coffee, nurturing me.

I do not like the real macho types—that turns me off no end. But I do like interesting enough men who are not afraid to admit they have both feminine and masculine sides. I find myself most comfortable with men who are comfortable with having a very strong feminine side.

I've found that usually the real macho types are scared to death to talk about their male/female aspect. We all do have both. I think there's a male/female percentage that each of us has. That's just the way we were born. There are some women who are very masculine, some men who are very feminine.

When you look at it in terms of nature, you see everything has a range like that, the bell-shaped curve. So why not sexuality? There's some who will reverse, like the gays. Then there are bisexuals, some on either side, average people in the middle.

It's the same with the sex drive, on that curve. And it's no different than some people being morning people, some night people. Some need eight hours sleep, some need two. It doesn't make one better or worse. It just is.

I put myself as average on the libido scale. I've always been able to turn it off and turn it on. If I'm not in a relationship, I'm not even really too much aware of a sex drive, except when I was a teenager. If I'm in a relationship, I'm very aware and very interested in my sex drive. When I'm not, it isn't at the forefront of my mind. I just don't feel the urges ... they are just not there. Now that I'm taking medication, there's no sex drive at all.

***

To the young women of today, first of all I would say—sex is a wonderful thing, but you have to get to know the person first. Don't do it with just anybody. Find somebody you can trust. The only way you know that, is by spending time with him.

If you meet somebody on Saturday and by Sunday you think you know him, it probably isn't going to happen. Once in a while, you could be really lucky. In reality, the chances of that happening are pretty slim. The person who promises to be your one and only and take care of you for the rest of your life and do all these wonderful things ... be careful.

Also, nowadays you have an element of safety you must deal with. We thought it was bad in the 70s when all we had to worry about was the occasional case of the clap, or a venereal disease. That was it. They were fixable and reasonably quick fixes, too. Nowadays—Hello!—HIV is not something to laugh at. It's a helluva way to die. A friend of mine, a person I worked with, I hear he ended up totally blind and in agony. A young guy, too. I wouldn't want that for anybody.

Safety is a serious issue. I don't happen to feel this is somehow God coming down, sending HIV as punishment for doing this stuff—that's crap. Also that it's a gay disease, that's crap too. Nonetheless, there are consequences that are life threatening and life changing events. That's a big price to pay for momentary pleasures ... especially if it's with somebody who didn't give a shit about you to begin with.

Talking is important. Some people are so afraid of even talking about sex. You don't want to clinically beat it to death, but I think a lot of positive things can happen when you do talk about it. Women used to think, 'Oh my god, I must be sick because ...,' but really that was only because they didn't talk to each other. find out what was really going on.

Then the Catholic Church used to say if you masturbated you'd go to hell. All these myths and stories going around and nobody knew what was real and natural. Education is the key.

In the Victorian era, for my grandmother, if a woman liked sex and said so, she was automatically a very bad girl ... just because she liked it. I think that's changing. You see women now in relationships not being totally knocked down because they enjoy sex. I can't see a woman in the 18th century going around saying 'I really like sex.' Even if she was married and only had sex with her husband, she couldn't say it.

I think discussing sex has some very positive effects and may save a lot of people from making a lot of bad mistakes, too.

Women's sexuality is very much involved with nurturing. And certainly we could use a hell of a lot more nurturing in this society—for ourselves and each other and the men. I look at men—they are still being raised in different ways than girls.

The thing I've always been very shocked about is ... supposedly the ideal relationship is a woman and a man. Since men and women think so different-ly, why aren't there mandatory courses to understand the opposite sex, with whom you're supposed to spend the rest of your life?

Why don't we have courses on marriage in high school? You still don't need any kind of education in order to get married or have a child. I'd love to see some concerted effort to fill that gap. Planned Parenthood has done some very positive things educating people about birth control. We need more programs like that around sex and marriage.

I see women talking more together and working more together and I think that is one of the reasons women have gotten more pull, more power. There's something about women, once they get passed 55, there's a real kinship. Like all of a sudden we belong to the old crony club. And it's real—a willingness to support each other, to help each other, to talk to each other. I don't see that among young women.

I see it over and over again ... like I'll be in the bathroom, at work, and all the fifty year olds are laughing and talking about sex. You all of sudden can get interested in this club. At the same time you also become very invisible to the male population—actually the male and female population—under fifty.

Before I was fifty, I could walk into a store and the sales people would say, 'Oh can I help you?' Now when I walk in, I see them but they just don't see me anymore. It's really interesting and bizarre. But yet we're all still sexual beings. People at one time were convinced that after fifty, you didn't do anything.

It will be interesting to see what will happen in the next phase of our development. I want to come back in 5000 years and see if there's any difference. Part of me would like to see some difference. Part of me is very concerned that, while outwardly it will be a little different, the same problems still exist, like we haven't grown at all.

I really think women can grow and be good teachers, if only we can get the men to pay attention. The sad part is, if there was real cooperation, can you imagine what this race could do? It would really be heaven on earth if we cooperated with each other ... just especially because we have different strengths—that's why it could be so good.

# 15

# Marianne

I really didn't encounter the whole good girl/bad girl paradigm. I was the class clown, so I kind of fell outside the whole paradigm, although I tended more toward the bad girl because I was disruptive. I would do anything for a laugh. When I was in grade school, it was pretty common for boys to be clowns but not all that common for girls.

I had a very emotionally unavailable mother, so I had to manage my mother's emotions about my behavior. Then I learned pretty early on that if I kept up really good grades and measured up, I could pretty much do whatever the hell I wanted.

In some ways I had the freedom I saw boys having in families. I didn't have brothers so I had no comparison within the family. I just didn't have to deal with my parents going, 'Oh you're not supposed to do this, you're not supposed to do that,' because I really knew how to play the game. Keep my grades up, be really productive and then whatever I did in my free time was none of their business. That was really helpful.

I remember experimenting with sex really early on. I masturbated and I remember having an orgasm when I was about four because I discovered my father's lazy boy reclining chair had a vibrator in it. I straddled the arm and I got off. Wow! I was very aware and orgasmic at a very early age.

I remember experimenting with girls really early on too. And boys. I think I'm one of those people who really didn't have a preference. I was very lonely. My sisters were seven and fourteen years older than I was—we lived on a farm so any contact I had with other kids was pretty rare. I was as interested in girls as I was boys, but I didn't have a preference one way or another.

I remember chasing this one little boy down to the point where I probably frightened him forever. I would lay in wait for him. I loved him so much I would ambush him. I made him wet his pants once because I jumped out from between some cars. It was horrible. Poor little Robert Churchill. I remember lying in bed at night and just thinking about these guys. We were maybe seven?

I loved being in love. We had a big make out party, when I was nine, at the piano teacher's house. When the adults were gone, their daughter had this party and we made out with all the boys, then we tried making out with each other. I was always real willing to experiment with anybody. I really don't ever remember thinking about the good/bad paradigm. I remember having it as private, none of my parents' business. I didn't feel ashamed. I think they liked it that way.

At school, I noticed the girls who were developing and was mortified because I wasn't. I have very keen memories of my childhood. In junior high, there were a couple of girls we stayed away from because they were greasers. That's how we identified bad girls—as greasers. South and North Dakota had enclaves of all northern Europeans, with hardly any southern Europeans. They are states with very little population. The way people made people wrong in those communities was by religion.

The most exotic people to us were Roman Catholic Irish. They were very rare, so they were called greasers, too. We didn't have any African Americans, Italians, Mexicans or Latin Americans. We had one Jewish family in town. One. They had to drive 300 miles one way—600 miles round trip—to go to synagogue. We are talking about a very homogenous society, with Norwegians and Swedes making each other wrong. Two brands of white bread.

As far as homogenous in our little towns—my mother and her sister happened to be relatively dark skinned. They were teased unmercifully for being less than the whitest of the white. Talk about a stretch. They were mortified and would wear gloves and hats and bathe themselves in buttermilk to try to bleach their skin, they got teased so badly about it.

The whole good/bad thing wasn't very present. High school was not in my town. I got caught breaking and entering, because I was out of control. I was a straight A student and I got caught. My parents were freaked out. I went to my father and said, 'I have to get out of here, go to another city or I will end up killing Mom.' By that time I was so emotional and she was so flat line. She never talked to me.

So he took that seriously. I wrote away for private schools. And I found one for kids who were in trouble and missionary kids. It was a Lutheran boarding school about 300 miles from our town. Again I was such an overachiever, head of the debate team, primary person in the theatre department, winning debate tournaments but I'm also tripping on acid while I'm doing it. I had this thing going where I just pretty much did whatever I wanted to do. My parents weren't there and the dorm people didn't know what I was doing.

We didn't talk sex much in the dorm. We literally had a mix of girls from all over the world—missionary kids, pastor's kids in trouble, behavior problems. I fit right in, but mostly because I was so bored with public schools. Now when I look back on it, I was something of an adrenaline freak. I loved doing things that were exciting. I obviously wouldn't have talked about it then. I was also very proud of it.

*** 

I was sexually active then. The school was coed. I made love for the first time when I was twelve, in a tree house with this boy that I loved—he was a greaser. It scared the hell out of me ... I liked it but I was very aware I could have gotten pregnant. I made a pact with God that if I wasn't pregnant, I would abstain from sex until I was sixteen. I still did heavy petting and lots of oral sex.

Four months before my sixteenth birthday, I skipped school, took a bus to the next bigger town, randomly picked a doctor's office from the phone book—in order to get birth control—because I knew I wasn't willing to have an out of wedlock baby. I had plans and raising children wasn't in the plans. So I went and finally found one.

The first doctor tried to get sexual with me. I ran out of his office and found the second doctor, who gave me a lecture about Jesus. I ran out of that office and found another one. He said, 'I hope my daughters are as responsible as you are,' then gave me a one year supply of birth control pills—free!

When I look back on that and think about a fifteen year old being that responsible, I'm pretty impressed with myself.

So I started taking birth control pills. About ten days before my sixteenth birthday, I called a boy who had graduated a year earlier and moved to Minneapolis. I asked 'How would you like to make love to me for my sixteenth birthday?' I took a bus to Minneapolis and we made love. He was such a bad lover and it was a wretched disappointment.

He really didn't know what to do with me. He couldn't figure out if I was a good girl or a bad girl either. I was always confounding people because they couldn't categorize me. Obviously somebody on the deans' list, straight A student, a liberated teen girl—they couldn't put me anywhere. The Midwest was about ten years behind the coasts and I was behaving more coast than Midwest.

I graduated from high school at sixteen and came out to California when I was seventeen and I've been here every since. 'Oh, good, I'm home. This is where I'm supposed to be.' That was 1972. I was always a California girl, because it's actually a country, not a state.

\*\*\*

At eighteen, I saw myself as able and willing, and as horny as any man. I saw myself as an equal. I saw myself as responsible for my own sexuality. I had a vibrator and used it. I had my first hand vibrator when I was sixteen and pleasured myself with it frequently, not instead of men but just because I liked getting off.

When I was eighteen, I was in a dorm that was a suite, and I was this little vibrator maven. I asked all my girlfriends 'Have you ever had an orgasm?' 'What's that?' they would ask. I went, 'Oh my God, I have a treat for you.' I distinctly remember swabbing off my vibrator with alcohol and lending it to all the women in my suite, saying 'Look, this is what you do, you'll get off and you'll thank me years later.' I turned on about eight women to orgasms ... 'You don't know what an orgasm is?' I made myself into an orgasm missionary.

I had come to California because I had longings for a man. He was a teacher at my high school and he had been fired because of rumors we were sleeping together ... but we weren't. He was a real gentleman and he knew he was in a power position. He did not take advantage of me and we did not have sex. I would have done it, but he was too ethical. The rumors started anyway, and he was fired anyway. So he came out to Stanford to get his MFA in acting and I followed him out.

Within a half hour of being together, we discovered we desperately disliked each other—after a year and a half of longing and torrid phone calls, letters back and forth. We actually met, he picked me up at the bus station and it's like, uuuh, who are you? It was mutual. I haven't seen him since.

I've been trying to track him down because I want to tell him what an impact he had on my life. He was one of the only adults in South Dakota who said to me, 'Look, you're really smart, you're really talented. Get out of here.' I've often wondered, if I'd been a boy, would people have encouraged me to apply to Ivy League schools? I really was able and ambitious enough for that. He was one of the only adults I knew who said 'Get out of here, go east, go west, you're going to die here.' I would have been an alcoholic, probably playing the lottery as I smoked my cigarettes.

I was admitted to a theatre company at a small junior college in Santa Maria. It was considered the summer camp for the ACT Ashland Shakespeare actors. I got in and then I stayed on for the academic year and then I transferred on to UC Irvine.

I was almost always having an affair with a professor. I started a pattern. The guy in charge of the acting department directed three or four of the six shows we put on during the year. He and I fell in love with each other. He had just recently come out of a monastery, after ten years, and was a lot older than me. He was horny, I was horny, so it was a perfect match. I was just smitten.

Then he calls one day to tell me, 'I've got gonorrhea, which means you probably do too.' Here I am at eighteen, and I'm scared, because I don't remember if gonorrhea makes you crazy or kills you.

He says, 'I'm coming over because the County requires I make sure my partner gets treated.' So he arrives, honks the horn for me from the curb, and I see he's borrowed a station wagon. He's got two other girls in there. It was stunning. Stunning! I should have said, 'Fuck you, I don't think so.' But I got in the car obediently, we went and got our shots and that was it.

Next, I had an affair with an English professor in the same college. After that, when I transferred to UC Irvine, I was lovers with the head of the music department. He was married and I had enough of a feminist ethic to say, 'We can do this, but you need to assure me your wife knows about me.' So he took me home, I met her, we got to be friends. It was so California.

He just contacted me two weeks ago … and ironically, my husband used to work for him. He was the musical director for a famous comedy show, while doing the music professor thing at the same time. We used to fuck each other silly in his office, behind the desk, on the floor. It was so fun.

Occasionally I'd have a couple of lovers at the same time … because my main love was my career—that's what I wanted to do in life. I never hid anybody from anybody else—it always had to be above board. I really was not into sneaking around, mostly because I'm just a terrible liar. I've got too much going on in my life to manage lies. I felt so vulnerable in the area of sex, it felt like it was just not a cool thing to lie about.

After college I went to law school, starting in 1974 and finishing in 1977. I had multiple partners during law school. I couldn't handle a steady relationship. It was impossible, what with studying and passing the bar. That's where I met my first husband.

I was going to law school and also running a theatre company when I met him. So we got married. I had this glitch of, 'Oh my god, I don't think I can make it on my own, I need a partner.' I didn't marry him with the idea of starting a family—neither of us wanted children. We were really good friends and lovers. I was never unfaithful to him.

***

I was obviously orgasmic—I had lots of orgasms, but I've always wanted to actually study advanced sex, tantra stuff. I read books about it but I found the men I was with to be really reluctant to experiment. My first husband and I broke up because we didn't have sex for two years and I was like, 'This is not okay.' He wouldn't go to therapy, he just wouldn't, and he was not forthcoming about what was going on with him. We drifted apart.

He was a recording engineer in the rock and roll industry. He really was not into self-reflecting, into being open and honest about his most intimate things. I loved him a lot intellectually and politically we were just great for each other. We had the same sense of humor but, sexually ... he just was not very interested.

Part of it too was that he'd go to work at 5:30 in the evening and wouldn't get home until 5:30 in the morning. Then I'd be getting up to go to work, doing what I was doing, so we literally didn't know each other after awhile. But I didn't cheat on him.

I stayed single for awhile and had a few partners. I had one partner, this guy named John, who was like a Nordic god. As far as what I found attractive, the chemistry between us was great ... but we just almost killed each other. That sex was really really good, but otherwise the relationship was horrible. Even he wasn't into experimenting with where you could take sex, either.

So what made the sex with John so really good? High quantity, yes. It wasn't quality so much as how we completely turned each other on. We could just look at each other and be panting. But as far as technique goes, it wasn't there. It was just a real chemistry thing.

Then I met husband number two. That was highly charged sexually too. He was seven or eight years younger than I was and we were really hot for each other. I wasn't hip yet to the idea that, maybe, that wasn't the best way to start a relationship. It sounds so stupid now. We were very hot for each other but a terrible match. I ended up just intimidating the hell out of him, mostly because I had a lot more life experience. I was thirty-five at that time. We married in '88 and split up in '96. Eight years.

He told me, at one point, if I ever got fat he would leave me. So I went 'Oh yeah'—unconsciously, of course, and I got really fat ... 230 pounds. Later I lost all that weight.

***

Then in 1995 I went to Beijing as a delegate to the UN Conference on Women and also as a journalist. I met a woman there, and a year later we started being lovers. We lasted together for about eight years. It was a major relationship for me, but I don't call it a marriage because every time she said, 'Let's get married,' I didn't think so. Finally, in kind of a tiff, I had to say, 'I think I'm basically straight.' It was like coming out as a straight person. She was definitely into women and did not see men at all. That was never true for me.

She'd say 'Oh you're just a chicken, you're just afraid to come out.' But no, the truth was that it was just as difficult, if not more so, to be bisexual than to be gay, because the gay community is giving you shit and the straight community is giving you shit. So no, I'm not hiding anything.

I was always amazed at how intolerant the gay community was about bisexuality. I would say the majority of gay and lesbian people were very judgmental and shitty about bisexuality. 'Don't you get what you're doing?' I'd say to these people. They were really intolerant.

I was with her off and on for almost ten years—from 1996 to 2006. We lived together for four years, then apart for two years, then together again until it ended. But it was impossible. She was fourteen years older than me, a very socially high-class Mexican from a gentile yet poor family. All the other branches of her family were very rich, at the same time her family was expected to act like they were in that social class—not royalty but close.

We had bodyguards when we were in Mexico because her brother was running for a national office and the family was afraid somebody would kidnap us. They were rich, rich, rich.

I had this expectation that she would be as feminist as I was. But she really was more macho than any man I've ever been with. Possessive. Mean. Jealous of men, jealous of women. Here I was, this ardent feminist activist, well known in my field, with this woman who couldn't stand that I was doing anything but taking care of her. Good lord.

She wasn't willing to experiment sexually either—she was very conventional in many ways. She was willing, I guess, but nothing like tantric sex. The truth was, she really couldn't be bothered. Highly sexual, she wanted more sex from me all the time but wouldn't swing out of her own comfort zone. It was partially age—fourteen years between us was a big difference.

I loved her but, oh my god, what a terrible time. She was a therapist and bilingual but not bicultural. She was raised in Mexican, very Catholic ways. As a young woman she was in a very deep underground gay and lesbian subculture in Mexico City.

I wish she was a writer because her early life would be a fascinating novel. How they would sneak around and be with some of the movie stars of the time and how clandestine it had to be. Fascinating. That was her background. Me, I'm some South Dakota, solidly middle class, do-it-yourself kind of mentality. She always had servants—she treated me like a servant. I stuck it out for many years.

I'm very loyal. When I say I'm going to do something, I do it, even when I'm suffering. After two marriages, I wasn't going to do 'cut and run' again. I don't have kids. She had kids and grandchildren and I became part of that. I wasn't just leaving her, I was leaving the whole structure and social unit—that was heartbreaking. I finally had the strength to say, 'We're both suffering. Yuck.'

\*\*\*

Then I met Nate and he is a soul mate. We're just really happy with each other on all levels. We have great sex, a great relationship, we talk until late in the night like little girls at a slumber party.

Nate is the most willing to experiment sexually of any lover I've had. We went to a couple of tantric classes. Ironically, we're both not at our prime, by any stretch, as we start this work. The nice thing is, he doesn't care what my body looks like. He says, 'Oh you're yummy to me.' I'm used to being a size six. He doesn't care.

Sex is different than it was in the past. My body has changed. The first time we made love, he tore me because I hadn't had sex with a man in five years and I had dried up in ways I wasn't aware of. I'm through menopause now and on a low level hormone. After toughing it out for years I finally said I'm going to do some hormones for awhile. So I'm sleeping again. I'm not into suffering for more years. No more—period.

And he's dealing with no drive. So we're both dealing with getting older. It used to be I would be panting if somebody looked at me a certain way and that is no longer true. I miss that, too. I miss being really horny.

***

Since menopause, I would say that quantity hasn't changed, because Juanita and I, as well as Nate and I, have sex about once a week. In terms of quality? Boy, comparing a woman to a man as a lover? That's not easy. And then comparing men to men? I was pre-menopausal with her and post-menopausal with Nate. I've never articulated the differences and don't know if I can.

I've actually been trying to come every day with a vibrator—just to keep active and to keep those juices flowing. And I do 30 to 100 Kegals a day. My sister, who is fourteen years older than I am, is having some bladder issues and I thought maybe I could head some of that off. We have very similar bodies.

One of my dear friends, a woman named Gail who is over eighty, walks around saying 'An orgasm a day keeps the doctor away.' I think she's right. So I take my vitamins and I have my orgasm every day. I'm experimenting with myself to see if it takes longer to get off. Yes, it does, but the quality of the orgasm is still there. Maybe not the length of time I feel it.

I'm using myself as a lab rat, in some ways, to see if it's possible to obtain the orgasmic intensity I had when I was having my period. I haven't arrived at any conclusions yet. Since it's only been in the last century that most of us live past 35 or 40, we're pioneers in a lot of ways. Our longevity has extended so far so fast

***

I can only surmise why all my partners before Nate weren't interested in studying sex … because they really didn't want to discuss it. If they did talk about it, it was in the most cursory of terms. There just seemed to be a lack of curiosity. And they invariably interpreted my bringing it up as a complaint about them and their sexual 'prowess.' I just want to see what authentic human sexual potential is. They took that as being dissatisfied, which I wasn't. I just wanted to know.

Non-orgasmic women will often fake it because that's what their partners want to believe. But I've only faked it once or twice with somebody because I wanted to get it over with and knew I wasn't going to pursue a long term relationship with that person.

With my solid partners, I've never lied because I don't think it's fair. And, they don't learn about my body. So if I'm faking an orgasm, how are they going to learn what gets me off? On the contrary, I have actively trained them. This doesn't feel good, this feels good. Yeah, I did and do that. And they were amenable to that.

***

My hottest experience sexually was very hot. I was nineteen and my father was the head of a big insurance company. We were at a Board meeting in Yellowstone, at this beautiful lodge. All the members of the Board of Directors brought their families. There was a huge formal dinner. One of the sons was sitting right across from me. We looked at each other and it was like an, 'Oh my god,' experience.

I wrote my room number on a slip of paper and slipped it to him as I left, after dessert. I left my room door ajar and he slipped in. We made hot passionate love without ever saying a word to each other. And he slipped out and we never saw each other again. That was really hot.

It wasn't a fantasy. It was real. It was pretty amazing. Completely animal hot, two young animals.

I fantasize when I masturbate. I occasionally fantasize when we're making love, although I'm pretty present with a lover. I suppose the fantasy is more about imagining people watching. It's one of those things I would never ever do, so it's really absolutely in the fantasy realm.

I love the physical sensation of sex, but mostly I love the intimacy of it, being close. My mom did not physically interact with us, never hugged or kissed us or anything. I just think I've been starving for physical contact my entire life.

That's one of the things I love about Nate. He's so huggy … warm and round. I love the smell of him and the tactile skin to skin thing. There's nothing I don't like about it. I love the unabashed pleasure, the sounds, the verbal play. I love all of it.

What I don't like about post-menopausal sex is feeling like I gotta schedule it or make time for it or be so intentional about including it. I think I could go for months now without having sex and then I would say, 'Oh, no, we forgot to have sex.' So it's not on some kind of chemistry schedule anymore, so I need to plan it like theatre. I don't like that part, right now.

I think what's most endearing is a lover who loves what you're doing. I love giving Nate head. He's just so happy when I do and he's so happy to be with a woman who loves it and clearly he's never been with a woman like me before. His experience is with women who act like they're doing him a favor. But with me, he sees that it gives me as much pleasure as it gives him. He's just so appreciative. I don't know if that's a habit but it's clearly endearing and such a delight for me.

When you talk about annoying habits, this occurred to me because it made me laugh. On a marquee on Wilshire Boulevard, I read, 'I fake foreplay.' I don't know if it was a play but it just struck me as so funny. I thought, okay, a guy's form of faking orgasm is faking foreplay. So I guess if I find anything annoying it would be, kinda, what's the rush? Let's do this like a dance ... or a dinner. We don't have to get to the main course immediately. Can we have some hor d'ouvres and some wine first?

*** 

I think the whole good girl/bad girl idea is a concept of the patriarchy that I never bought into. The whole Madonna/whore template has served a lot of purposes—including keeping women from relating to one another as human beings. And to keep women at arm's length from one another so we won't share what's going on about sex in general.

I read **Sisterhood Is Powerful** when I was fifteen. I don't remember the details but I remember saying, 'Jeez, this is a rigged game' and I understood a whole lot then about how the world works.

So it just felt so wrong to me to see women as competitors, or to put us into this good/bad framework. That's not how people are. Nobody's good or bad, we're all all of it. I think I've lucked out in that way ... not that I'm not impacted by that concept, because I am, just like everyone else.

It's in the culture. It's not like one person can take on an entire culture. But you can certainly be aware of it and call it out, not buy into it. That doesn't mean it's not there. I really think a lot of the good/bad stuff for women has now shifted from sex to the shape of our bodies.

I work with women trying to integrate mind/body/spirit. A lot of women are deeply separated from their bodies. So now I think we've shifted into, 'You're a good woman if you're thin and slender. You're a bad woman if you're fat.' It's probably from the so called sexual revolution—which is a whole different conversation.

A lot of women internalize 'good' as being the way the media portrays women. And whatever that way is, defines what a right woman is. So as far as women's sexual behavior goes, some of the onus has come off sexuality but shifted onto physical presentation. I have yet to make peace with that.

I'm a person of the media. First of all, middle-aged women are not very well represented ... especially chubby middle aged women. We don't see them. So okay, I like the way I eat, I like my body. But I can wave my tv career goodbye if I don't get these thirty pounds off.

Only part of me says I'm not bad because I'm fat. I think I really dodged the bullet with the good/bad sexual stuff but not with the body image stuff. In general, we're pretty invisible. That's my experience.

\*\*\*

If I had words of wisdom for daughters and granddaughters, I would say, first of all, study oxytocin ... it will clear some mystery about why you're attracted to some men who are clearly inappropriate for you.

And oxytocin being what it is, I see now why I bonded with some men that were not good for me. Well, we had an orgasm together so that bonded me to them and made me yearn for them. I really didn't take into account all the other factors that make for a good relationship. It's not that it's not important to be attractive, it's just that oxytocin is so powerful, you'll bond with somebody even if he clearly doesn't have your best interests in mind.

You and your pleasure are the most important factors in all of it. If you have to put up with something or you're doing something that does not give you pleasure, do not do it. By the same token, if you're doing something that gives you pleasure, keep on.

What if ultimately our highest calling is enjoying our lives? What if?

# Part III

# She Learns

*' "One day in your wineshop, I drank a little wine,*
*and threw off this robe of my body,*
*and knew, drunk on you, the world is harmony.*
*Creation, destruction, I am dancing for them both." Rumi*

*'So sacred art and dance demand action from within the ground of*
*our being; it demands a return to that Divine Silence from which*
*the art came; it demands as profound an act of*
*receptivity as we can make and as profound an act of*
*responsibility as we can make. Because receptivity has to lead to re-*
*sponsibility, if it isn't to be decadent.*

*' "The purpose of language," Rumi says, "is to show you*
*something far off, something moving, trembling in the distance,*
*like a heat merage." '*

Andrew Harvey, *The Way of Passion*

# 16

# From Quantity to Quality

In Part 1, we looked at the prevailing wisdom around woman's sexuality at mid-twentieth century and her innate sexual capacity, compared to sexually reproducing females in nature. In Part 2, fourteen women tell their stories of participating in and living through a potentially profound sexual revolution for women. Part 3 now focuses on analysis and synthesis, teasing out of their collective stories a picture of how the opening dance steps in this phase of the woman's revolution played out in their lives and its implications for future generations of women dancing the next round.

This next chapter analyzes what the women said about these issues and how they played out in each stage of a woman's life—maiden/virgin, matron/mother, and crone/wise woman.

One caveat. I resist destroying the gestalt of each woman's story by picking it apart or distorting it with statistics. While percentages can tell us how many women did or didn't do something, only the stories tell us why. Because fourteen is too small a sample to say anything definitive about all women, you get the stats merely to show what was normal or average among this group of Boomer women.

## Maiden/Virgin

Girls in the 1950s were, by and large, carefully coached in good girl/bad girl behavior. Some remember hearing the lessons as early as four years old.

At home, many heard it first from their parents, especially their mothers. Some told their daughters 'you will be bad if you do or don't this or that,' while other mothers wouldn't say what exactly was bad. One woman remarked, "My mother didn't have to say anything, you just knew what was bad by how she acted." Other women claimed they were still hearing a mother's voice, well after they had left home.

At the same time, almost all reported that their parents never actually talked to them about sex. Few girls were allowed any information about their own bodies or their periods—most received only a brief talk from their mothers after they had started bleeding. The primary message was that periods just had to be endured. Annie Laurie, Eva and others spoke of sneaking around to read books and look at pictures about the body.

**Interview Questions:**

In your childhood, while you were growing up, did you encounter good girl/bad girl training?

What was your definition of good girl/ bad girl?

Which did you consider yourself, good or bad?

How were you raised to think about sex? Was it talked about at home? How was it dealt with?

At age 18, how did you see yourself sexually?

None of the ladies learned about the wonder and mystery of their bodies and of childbearing. Even those with older sisters said no one talked about sex and girls' bodies at home. Several mentioned that the messages in their homes came from Victorian-thinking grandmothers—the primary message being that liking sexual pleasure is forbidden to girls.

At the same time, almost half experimented sexually as children—touching themselves, touching and being touched by others. One woman described her first orgasm at four, while another said she experimented with intercourse at five.

Four out of the fourteen women were abused physically and/or sexually—mostly by fathers. Two escaped the home as soon as they could, to get away from it.

On the schoolyard, kids enacted the myth by labeling some girls good and some bad, based on how they walked or talked or the clothes they wore. Only one woman, Lily, mentioned that boys could be bad too and were therefore more appealing to her. Two grew up in towns that were so small, and ruled by so many churches, that no one had to mention good girl/bad girl at all. Instead, girls were looked down on because their skin wasn't white enough, or they were Irish Catholic greasers—that was enough.

In high school, several women were envious of the bad girls—wanting to know what the bad girls had already learned about sex—mainly how it actually felt. A few figured out how to be bad girls without anyone knowing.

Katarina, Lyla and Marianne felt the least influence from the myth, mostly because they were not concerned with what others thought.

---

### Thread: Good girl/ bad girl myth

29%—none or minor influence

21%—major influence

50%—significant influence

---

Lyla, strongly influenced by her religious upbringing, was guilt free and clear that no one else could judge her. Katarina became a bad girl—sexually active—and also guilt-free and happy. Marianne finessed her situation by being so accomplished in school and out, that no one noticed as she did exactly as she pleased.

The myth was clearly pervasive—71% said the myth defined their growing up, while 50% felt that effect had significantly influenced their behavior.

At the same time, all the women but one, Carla, who had been raped, deliberately chose when they would lose their virginity—most using high school graduation as the benchmark. No one was still a virgin when she married, despite their cultural programming to wait for Mr. Right.

Most lost their virginity before their eighteenth birthday—57%. Three turned eighteen first and three more were older than that. The youngest deflowering was at twelve years old while the oldest was twenty-one. The average age the girls chose was seventeen.

The subject of guilt came up a lot, but usually it wasn't from a sense of *being* a bad girl and therefore guilty. It was more from the fear of getting pregnant or disgracing their families. At that age, they seemed to interpret a reprieve from pregnancy as a reprieve from the 'sin' of sex itself.

When asked how they would rate themselves—good or bad girls—only three clearly believed they had behaved as good girls—Stephanie, Akulina and Marianne. Four said the concept itself just hadn't been part of their thinking. The remaining seven ladies seemed truly conflicted—feeling they had been very good and very bad—both were true about them.

I asked all the ladies how they saw themselves sexually, at eighteen, figuring that birthday is a rite of passage for girls on the threshold of womanhood and independence from parents. Except for Katarina and Eva, they seemed confused by the question, as if, at that age, they really had no concept of themselves sexually—sex was for the fun of doing it, not stepping back to view it intellectually.

***Thread: Religion***

9—major influence in life

5—minor or no influence

2—still active in a church

It was fun, it felt good, they were given the Pill by the gods and there weren't really any other considerations.

## Mother/Matron

For most of these ladies, the meat of their stories happened during their matron/mother years. They answered the first, open-ended question, mostly in terms of the relationships they had with partners—marriages, divorces, lovers. Unbidden, they answered many of the other questions along the way.

The good girl/bad girl concept rarely surfaced during this time in the women's lives. Most said all their guilt about sex went away as soon as they married. I heard in their answers the assumption that they were women and 'women are sexual—well, duh. So what?'

They saw their sexual freedom—the innate right to choose to say yes or no—as natural, along with the responsibility for any consequences. Many shared stories about the mistakes they had made along the way—choosing wrong partners, mistaking an oxytocin high for love, situations that didn't work out, etc.—all of which they saw, with wisdom, as just another part of learning and growing.

The myth of Mr. Right was deeply engrained. All but one woman married, at least once. Collectively, they married twenty-three times and divorced fourteen times.

They saw a connection between marrying for sex, then realizing the rest of the marriage didn't work and they needed to get out of it. By the same token, marrying for security, to escape, or because it was accepted that you would/should—these marriages also ended in divorce.

Only one of the fourteen women, Stephanie, is still married to her first husband. She emphasized how important it had been to her that the mate she chose was a friend first—someone she could trust for the long haul and as a daddy.

All but two women spoke openly about her ability to orgasm during masturbation. For most of them, orgasming with a partner is much harder, requiring time and patience. Most felt the orgasms didn't happen because their partner was in a hurry and unwilling to spend the time she needed to be fully aroused and satisfied.

The women also thought they often needed more trust in a lover or situation, in order to fully relax and enjoy themselves sexually. Three women spoke of feeling raped as an adult, eleven did not.

---

### *Interview Questions:*

What happened next, after you turned 18?

How many men have you made love with? Was it satisfying? Did you orgasm?

Were you monogamous in your committed relationships?

Did you masturbate?

What is your hottest fantasy?

What was your hottest sexual experience?

What do you like about sex? What don't you like? What won't you do?

What is the most annoying habit you've experienced with a lover?

What is the most endearing habit you've experienced with a lover?

Did you talk to your children about sex?

---

Three women volunteered that they had faked orgasms. Since the question wasn't asked, we don't know how many others have or still do fake it. Marianne said she wouldn't consider faking it because 'how else would he learn to do it right?'

All but one woman admitted to masturbating. Those who had found out about vibrators early on, were very positive about its benefits. They believed that masturbating and using a vibrator helped them to become multi-orgasmic later on with a partner.

Like most of us, they were curious to know how they compared with other women—handling situations, orgasming/not orgasming, were they different, better or worse? Some had talked with girl friends and felt strongly about the value of women actually talking to each other.

Nine out of fourteen women reported they had experienced multiple orgasms and prolonged ecstatic states, '…until I was so full of oxytocin I couldn't walk.' Six of those women said they had had relationships where multiple and/or extended orgasms were normal sex for them.

They described the prolonged ecstatic state as mystical—esoteric, spiritual—a qualitatively different experience from a normal or average orgasm.

A few women shared a defining event, when a skillful lover had come along and opened them up sexually. They called the event an epiphany and life-changing, especially to their self-esteem. All nine women expressed deep gratitude and joy that they had experienced such a lover.

### Thread: Did you/do you orgasm?

| | | |
|---|---|---|
| Yes, when masturbating | 13 | 93% |
| Yes, with a partner | 8 | 57% |
| Only rarely or sometimes with a partner | 4 | 29% |
| Never with a partner | 2 | 14% |
| Orgasm is always harder with a partner than when masturbating | 12 | 79% |
| Multiple orgasms/prolonged ecstatic states—at least one experience | 9 | 64% |
| First orgasm is harder than the following orgasms | 9 | 64% |

The women were of two minds about the role of oxytocin in all that ecstasy. On the one hand, you feel *really good* when your body is full of it. On the other hand, it is easy to confuse oxytocin-induced cuddle /bonding, with love, compatibility or even friendship. They recommended getting to know what was real about one's own body around oxytocin.

Six women admitted enough curiosity to deliberately experiment with learning about her own sexual capacity. Some really wished they had started learning about sex when younger and randier. For the rest, the unspoken assumption seemed to be that you learned as you went along and that was good enough.

Some of the reasons they cited for not studying sex, besides lack of time or interest, included the reluctance of partners to consider change, and the assumption that her desire to know more about sex automatically meant either she's a slut or the partner is sexually deficient.

| Thread: | Children | Abortions |
|---------|----------|-----------|
| One | 2 | 1 |
| Two | 6 | 1 |
| Three | 2 | 0 |
| None | 4 | 12 |
| **Total:** | **20** | **3** |

Only two women trained a partner to better understand and satisfy her body. They both talked about the need for women to get beyond the barriers of a partner's vulnerability about his sexual prowess. As one woman said, taking control of the sexual situation and being willing to help him learn is the responsible thing to do.

Two women considered themselves skillful lovers. The women who had found or trained a skillful partner/lover, tended to marry them and keep them.

Libido is sometimes a murky concept, often misused. Because most women rarely talk about how often they want or actually have sex, it is difficult to compare oneself and know what is really a low, average or high libido, as in 'Am I normal?.' In the interviews, most of the women used the term to mean their perceptions of how much sex drive they had. Two women described themselves as having a relatively low libido; seven thought they were pretty average; and five gave themselves a high rating.

| Thread: | Libido |
|---------|--------|
| Low | 2 |
| Medium | 7 |
| High | 5 |

---

### Thread: Times married

| | |
|---|---|
| Once | 7 |
| Twice | 3 |
| Three times | 2 |
| Four times | 1 |
| Never | 1 |

*13 women collectively
married 23 times.*

### Thread: Times divorced

| | |
|---|---|
| Once | 5 |
| Twice | 3 |
| Three times | 1 |
| Never | 5 |
| [Widowed | 2 |
| Same partner | 2] |

*9 women collectively
divorced 14 times*

---

I assigned each woman a score of one to ten, based on her whole profile, for being sexually exper-ienced. My profile included number of partners, what they would or wouldn't do sexually, how they talked about their own sexuality, willingness to explore and/or experiment. This scale is very subjective and only useful in broad brush strokes.

Those women with children all said they had attempted to talk

Five women had experimented in lesbian relationships, while only one of those stayed in a long-term relationship. All five women viewed themselves as basically heterosexual.

None of the women who had *not* been monogamous expressed guilt about it. It wasn't even an issue in their youthful casual relationships. Those who were unsatisfied sex-ually in a committed relationship and then strayed, felt justified in their choices. Their reasons included a partner's prolonged illness, a partner's lack of skill as a lover and the immanent end of the relationship, reflecting similar reasoning prevalent among men.

Six women became happily monogamous as they matured and found Mr. Right, or said they would be if and when they found him, citing a long-term monogamous relationship as the most fulfilling sexually. Those who are in a monogamous situation now, all seem thankful to have a relationship that satisfies them.

---

### Thread:  Monogamous in a committed relationship?

| | Yes | No |
|---|---|---|
| Then (youth) | 5 | 9 |
| Now | 11 | 3 |

---

to them about sex … with more or less success. By the time the kids were teenagers, they didn't see their mothers as a primary source for information about sex.

Throughout the questions about likes and dislikes, the women liked affection and intimacy the most, being hurried or forced the least. Tenderness, compassion and a sense of humor went a long way toward making a lover endearing. Rushing to intercourse or ejaculation topped the list of annoying habits of lovers.

Every woman who experienced multiple and prolonged orgasmic states cited her partner's willingness to slow way down, put his full attention on her, take his time.

None of these women enjoyed pain as a path to pleasure, also rejecting exhibitionism, multiple partners and bondage.

| Thread: | Sexually experienced | # of partners | |
|---------|----------------------|----|----------|
| Low | 2 | 8 | (<10) |
| Medium | 8 | 4 | (11-100) |
| High | 4 | 3 | (101-200) |

| What women say about sex: | |
|---|---|
| **They find endearing:** | love, a call the next day, a sense of humor, dancing first, tenderness, no neediness, empathy, compassion, gentleness, lasting long enough for me to be fully aroused, laughter, affection, holds my face tenderly, touching and affection outside bedroom, intelligence, loving what I do to him, being nurtuing/nurtured, an excellent kisser, the right (natural) smell, talking to me during sex, having fun, goofing around, caring if I'm having a good time |
| **They find annoying:** | talking on phone during sex, domination, premature insertion, body odor, refusal to learn from women, rushing to ejaculation, farts, pushing my head on his cock, won't/doesn't listen, starts too fast, sloppy kissing, selfishness, stupid behavior, porn during sex, violence, 'I fake foreplay' attitude, rushing too much, lack of cleanliness, wham bam thank you ma'am, no intimacy, expectations, fantasizing during sex |
| **They like most:** | oxytocin, primitive feelings, breast fondling, foreplay, being sensual, laughter, affection, snuggling, kissing, afterwards, whole nights together, anticipation, intimacy, it's relaxing and reduces stress, a sense of connection, hugging, smell/scent, skin to skin, sounds, verbal play, talking, experiencing Sacred/God, just barely touching, dedication to my satisfaction, vagina as sacred mystery, gentleness, tenderness, makes my body run better, giving head |
| **They like least:** | wet spots, semen, answering phone during sex, penetration, no affection, hitting, spanking, hurrying, expectations, ickiness, oral sex, tongue down my throat, being forced, feeling used, he's too fast |
| **They won't do:** | s&m, exhibitionism, multiple people/couples, porn, spanking, sodomy, oral sex, bondage |

---

### *Thread: Good girl concept today:*

Same as always—based on strict father model

Not very useful concept in the course of their lives

Body shape more important than authentic
  sensuality

Girls sexualized too young

Media controlled—sexuality itself trivialized

---

---

### *Thread: Professions represented*
### *in the research group:*

| | |
|---|---|
| Teacher | Artist |
| Writer | Receptionist |
| Masseuse | Legal Secretary |
| Healer | Caregiver |
| Physician | Business manager |
| Educator | Office worker |
| Accountant | Movie producer |
| Secretary | Lawyer |
| Actor | Business Analyst |

---

## Crone/Wise Woman

Nine of the fourteen women are currently single. Five are married. The youngest was 52 at the time of the interview, the oldest was 66. The average age was 59.

Three of the women were retired, one semi-retired—she's flirting with going back to work. The other ten are active working professionals.

All the women still see themselves as sexual beings, each active in her own way, even the two women on medications, and the seven who reported themselves as mainly celibate right now. All five married women say they remain sexually active, with some changes, noted below. Three of the fourteen are still actively hoping to find a *right* partner.

Almost half the women said their libido had increased post-menopause, two said it was the same, while seven

### Interview Questions:

How do you see yourself sexually now? As a lover?

Do you orgasm?

Do you have a partner now? Are you sexually active?

How experienced do you see yourself sexually now?

How has sex changed for you over the years?

Did sex change for you pre- and post-menopause?

What do you think now about the good girl/bad girl concept?

How would you define a good girl today?

Any words of wisdom for the daughters and granddaughters out there?

women—only half—felt a lowered libido. Most were happy with what they had been dealt, or at least were content.

Many felt the transition to post-menopause had been smooth as they experienced less fear around sex itself—pregnancy, periods, getting their needs met, all were no longer issues.

Most felt that, while the quantity of their orgasming had diminished a bit, the quality had either remained the same or gone up. No one claimed the quality had gotten less. Several were wistful that they no longer had a chemistry schedule for sex, but now need to deliberately put sex on the calendar.

All the single women said that orgasming and making love has a different significance now that they are older—considerations of relationship and quality are a higher priority than the sex act itself. They want the experience to include intimacy and trust, to mean more than when they were younger.

Several of the single women are content to live without a partner, unwilling to make an active effort—they say it is too difficult to find a mature man who is appropriate, and they are capable of meeting their own sexual needs. A couple of them are willing to consider a relationship with a younger man.

Most of the single women (and a few of the married ones) still masturbate—three believing that an orgasm a day is healthy and will keep her younger and more vibrant as she ages, juicy rather than dried up.

| Thread:  *Libido changes post-menopause* | |
| --- | --- |
| Libido up | 5 |
| Same | 2 |
| Libido down | 7 |
| Content with that | 10 |
| Unhappy about it | 2 |
| On medications | 2 |

## Wise Voices

We come now to the three meatiest questions asked in the interview:
- What do you think now about the good girl/bad girl concept?
- How would you define a good girl today?
- Any words of wisdom for the daughters and granddaughters out there?

Today, most of women believe the good girl concept is a politicized control mechanism of men—basically the same as it's always been. They did not believe that our society has changed much in the way the patriarchy attempts to domesticate girls. Even so, they radically transformed the way they define a good girl for today's world.

The media has become *the* major delivery mechanism of sexual messages, most of it so trivialized that women's sexuality is a commodity, to be bought and sold like any other commodity. Because the media is so visually oriented, the good girl concept has shifted to include the shape of her body and her presentation—'makeup and clothes make the woman'—with little consideration for actual sensuality. Little girls are sexualized by age five or six.

Bad girls continue to be punished for being true to themselves. If she steps 'over the line' she comes to a bad end and is judged harshly—she isn't true to her own nature, she uses sex for barter, control, revenge. The women interviewed, however, changed their description of a bad girl to reflect her responsibility. Several of the women clearly saw inappropriate sexual behavior on the part of young women as a consequence of the abuse they received as children, not as a choice the girls made.

On the other hand, good girls live by their values and principles, are responsible and ethical. In other words, good girls are the same as good boys, and should be judged by the same standards as are good men and women, rather than standards evolved out of gender politics.

The women were very harsh about the role of gender politics in the way we raise girls, recognizing that patriarchy and misogyny are institutionalized sexism in our society. A Christian heritage, from men, has created a core belief that a woman's body should always be mistrusted, even when used by men for their own satisfaction.

The women clearly believed that mistrust and competition between women for men is fomented by gender politics and the masks women are forced to wear. The reason, they said, is men's fear of performance comparisons that might lead to feelings of sexually inadequacy.

The women had lots of words of wisdom for young

---

### Thread: Wise women say bad girls:

Use sex for barter, revenge, control, greed

Are irresponsible sexually, especially with STDs

Are judged harshly

Should be viewed as wounded, injured children

Should be judged age-appropriately

---

### Thread: Prevailing good girl concept:

Same as always—based on strict father model

Body shape more important than sensuality

Girls sexualized too young

Media controlled—sexuality itself trivialized

Not very useful concept in the course of their lives

women just starting out sexually, clustering around two recommendations: 1) take the time to know yourself, and 2) enjoy your body and sex.

The importance of knowing oneself focused on how easy it is for a woman to give herself away to a lover, rather than be intimate enough with herself to know the difference between love, lust and liking, especially before marriage.

They also said that a woman needs to know herself sexually before she can really enjoy sex, that authentic sexual enjoyment and pleasure are her right, as long as she is responsible for her own sexuality. Being a joint, equal partner will bring the most satisfaction to the experience.

---

### Thread: The new good girl:

Is sexually responsible

Uses prophylactics

Makes choices and accepts the consequences

Gets herself educated

Enjoys sex, authentically

Lives by principles of honesty, openness and love

Recognizes her responsibility for her own sexuality and sexual fulfillment

Cultivates a high self-esteem

Knows what she wants and doesn't compromise

Is willing to see herself as bad in a particular situation but good overall

### Thread:  Wise women say gender politics:

Is institutionalized sexism

Reflects men's terror of women's sexuality

Reflects men's desire to blame their fear on the women

Is institutionalized in religion, controlled by men who want to control women

Keep women from trusting each other so women will compete for men and won't make performance comparisons about men

Protects men's egos from feelings of sexual inadequacy

## *Authentically get to know yourself:*

- Remain your own person

- Be healthy and enjoy who you are

- Develop a willingness to be intimate with yourself as well as your partner

- Find your own definition of good girl/bad girl and don't judge other people

- Explore and find what works for you

- Watch yourself and your own behavior as much as you watch his

- Have compassion for yourself in sexual relationships, even if you make a mistake

- Be responsible for meeting your own needs

- Don't be quick to give yourself away—not just your virginity

- Be sure of yourself before having sex, every time

- If you have strong feelings, follow your heart—it tells you something about yourself

- Find the people who love you unconditionally and stick with them

- Study oxytocin in your own body

- Talk about sex with a partner and other women to find out what's really going on

- Spend time getting to know yourself

## *Be true to yourself:*

- Be friends first, then lovers
- Let sex be fun
- Stay light hearted
- Sex is a divine gift, be sure to enjoy it
- Look for love, don't wait for it
- If it's good, get rid of any guilt
- Only do what gives you pleasure
- Watch out for AIDS/HIV and other STDs − sex can be dangerous
- Play with someone, and if it's good, keep playing
- Get as much as you can, give as much as you can
- Don't equate a man screwing you with him liking you
- Give sex advice to a man when he needs it, despite his ego-resistance
- Desire, like lightening, just comes--sometimes it's chemistry and you don't always have control over it--different from sexing, which is your decision
- The saucier you try to be, the more likely it will lead to impersonal sex
- Give up victimization in all areas of your life, especially in sex
- Get past the body image malarkey
- Be a joint, equal partner

# 17

# Daphne's Dilemma

*"Dancing is surely the most basic and relevant of all forms of expression. Nothing else can so effectively give outward form to an inner experience. Poetry and music exist in time. Painting and architecture are a part of space. But only the dance lives at once in both space and time. In it the creator and the thing created, the artist and the expression, are one. Each participant is completely in the other. There could be no better metaphor for an understanding of the ... cosmos.*

*"We begin to realize that our universe is in a sense brought into being by the participation of those involved in it. It is a dance, for participation is its organizing principle. This is the important new concept of quantum mechanics. It takes the place in our understanding of the old notion of observation, of watching without getting involved. Quantum theory says it can't be done. That spectators can sit in their rigid row as long as they like, but there will never be a performance unless at least one of them takes part. And conversely, that it needs only one participant, because that one is the essence of all people and the quintessence of the cosmos."*

Lyall Watson, *Gifts of Unknown Things*

My two initial questions in this study were—what changes endured for the women, from the good girl myth to free love and on into maturity? Do these changes constitute the continuation of a real revolution, one that could radically change gender politics for future generations?

The women in this study dance in the footsteps of Suffragettes, Flappers and Rosie the Riveter in changing a woman's role in the world. Today's challenge is Daphne's dilemma—is it time yet? Can Daphne dance again, as her true self? Is it safe to start a new dance between men and women, one that is whole and authentic, sustainable for woman's (truly unique) sexual capacity, as well as man's?

Remember, it wasn't Daphne's choice to become frigid . . . she was poisoned. She protected herself from Apollo's urgent sexual need by growing a hard tree skin. Today, perhaps the dart and the danger have worn off and once again she can live in the profound sexual capacity Nature gives her.

Some of the women told me that participating in the interview changed their lives, shifting energy for them, opening their eyes to threads and patterns they hadn't paid attention to before. Some used the interview to say things to their lovers they couldn't or wouldn't say face to face. Others shed light for themselves on old dysfunctional patterns.

All of them were grateful for the opportunity to add their voices to the discussion because few thought the good girl myth was particularly useful in preparing them for real life. These women were amazingly consistent in their messages to young women of today—and to lovers.

That women are talking to each other at all about their sexual histories is a profound statement about changes in our society. That post-menopausal women are talking about prolonged ecstatic states is virtually unheard of, in ancient or modern literature.

The women lived through the Korean war, Cold War and Vietnam war, and started school learning to hide under their desks in case of nuclear war. They came of age while the Kennedy brothers and Martin Luther King were assassinated, the people in Watts rioted, People's Park erupted and students at Kent State were slaughtered by American troops – all on an early diet of the Mouseketeers, Bonanza and I Dream of Jeannie. It was a chaotic time in which to grow up.

While the women did not talk about these background events, the events affected the qualities of the women's liberation movement and sexual revolution of the 1970s, much as their parents were influenced and defined by the Great Depression and World War II.

The women also didn't directly address issues raised in Chapter 1. Most seemed unaware or unconcerned about the work of Kinsey or Masters and Johnson. None addressed her body in the context of nature, except for diminishing libido. Only Eva mentioned that ovulation and moon cycles affected her sexual desires. No one said they were aware of when they ovulated or that it was a problem or issue – Shlain's idea of hidden estrus. Most of those who had experienced prolonged orgasmic states were surprised by it, claiming they had never imagined it was possible.

All the women assumed they had the right to say no to sex whenever they wanted, even those who had been sexually abused as children. No one was still fighting that battle. In addition, no one talked about fear of dying in childbirth, although almost all had been seriously afraid of getting pregnant before they started using birth control.

Many had swept aside the constraints of good girl/bad girl with the advent of the Pill. If birth control was okay, then sex itself was okay, they reasoned. They openly exhibited sexual desire and behavior, discovered their clitorises and shopped around sexually for a mate.

### Starting a new dance

This is a radically different perspective from the world the women grew up in. I was struck by these points:

1. Over the course of their lives, most of the women had *not* found the prevailing good girl myth to be very useful.

2. They all agreed the new good girl takes the time to know herself and learns how to be responsible for her own happiness, is true to herself, *enjoys sex* and doesn't compromise on herself or her enjoyment of it.

3. Nine of the fourteen women report sexual capacities *way beyond* the ordinary orgasm.

4. Most report difficulty initially orgasming with a partner. They were both angry at partners for insufficient foreplay *and* defensive because their bodies weren't instantly ready—like a man's.

Let's look at each of these points a little closer.

*First,* the good girl myth wasn't useful. The women clearly saw it as a power play by male-dominated social institutions, especially churches. The myth focused on outward appearances such as clothes and talk. They were expected to live inside a mask by disconnecting from their bodies, without knowing what they were disconnecting from, to be ignorant and malleable, living in limbo between slave and goddess, wholly possessed.

Most lived the myth until sometime in their teens when it no longer resonated with a new set of core beliefs and root metaphors just emerging. Her body didn't *feel* like original sin. She didn't *feel* limited by traditional female roles. 'Go forth and multiply' no longer was the *only* path in front of her.

By early adulthood, the women knew that the myth hadn't prepared them with good decision-making skills around sex. The world was a different place. And, they had the Pill and didn't need those old judgments. As they took on more responsibilities in other areas of life, they also became more responsible for the consequences of their sexual behavior, gaining richer lives in the process. No one's story here was tragic. Society did not collapse because women took control of their bodies.

*Second,* they redefined a good girl myth that diametrically opposed the prevailing myth. Rather than taking on a mask imposed from without, their good girl goes deep within, authentically *knowing* who she is sexually and what fulfills her.

Then their good girl stays true to herself, is responsible for her sexuality without giving up enjoyment of her sexuality. She doesn't use people nor let herself be used sexually.

This is all so different from the prevailing myth. For 5,000 years, men have claimed the right to decide what fulfills a woman sexually, believing his satisfaction was more important than hers. After all, she is too irresponsible to be in control of her body, children or property, because she is physically weaker. 'To thine own self be true' really only applied to men. Girls should stay ignorant and naive, letting a man make decisions for her.

Without blinking, these wise women said pshaw to that, clearly seeing woman's values, responsibilities and abilities as equal to man's.

They did tell stories of oxytocin highs leading to some very ignorant decision-making . . . until they learned to recognize *that* melt-down and responded from their deeper goals. A woman who learns about her body is truer to herself, they said.

Collectively, the ladies in this project have 602 sexually active years. Their values are conscious, responsible, adult . . . polar opposite to the prevailing fears the good girl myth hides behind.

Why is this so profound? Because the wise women in this study fit into an 'average' range of sexual behavior—libido, marriages, divorces, children, lovers, careers—for their generation of Boomers, *and* they are living out a radically new story.

The women were clear—'Don't give yourself away before you even know who you are,' 'Define Mr. Right for yourself and make sure he's a friend to you,' 'Be in charge of your own life,' 'If you are going to have sex, only do it if it's fun for you,' 'You are responsible for your fulfillment' . . . in other words, 'To thine own self be true.'

The women did *not* transform their own lives after the 1970s into the titillation and trivialization of women's sexuality we see and hear in the media today—five media giants collectively did that. Instead, these women went deeper into themselves, figuring out what lifestyle worked for them, making changes, discovering new territory within, telling their daughters and granddaughters empowering stories.

Can we conclude that Daphne feels safe enough to morph back to her real form—of the senses, sexual?

*Third,* nine out of fourteen—67%—randomly selected post-menopausal women said they had experienced *prolonged orgasmic states* way beyond an ordinary orgasm. Two questions occur to me: 1) what is actually ordinary—the 11-second ordinary experience or the hours-long experience? And 2) the medical establishment claims 50% of women are non-orgasmic. Who's telling the truth here?

Do all women have the capacity for prolonged orgasming if two-thirds have the capacity? From Kinsey and others we know that early sexual behavior directly relates to later sexual capacity, so a woman's ability to experience prolonged ecstatic states might depend on how early she became sexually active, how many children she's had and how old she is now. At the same time, Eva was in her teens when she first experienced prolonged ecstasy.

We have no historical baseline on woman's higher-end orgasmic capacity, we only know what women are reporting today. It could be that women's sexual capacity is evolving because of improved health and longevity.

It could be that women have hidden it all along, like Daphne, during a 'might makes right' social mentality that left her feeling unsafe. It could be any number of things we don't see yet.

*Fourth*, most of the women were very defensive about how long it took them to get to the first ordinary orgasm. They described it as *difficult*, as if it should have been easier, taken less time. Compared to what?

They were angry with lovers who didn't take the time to get their momentum going, get them out of first gear. At the same time, they subtly judged themselves by how fast men are ready for intercourse.

Many men hold the point of view that women are deficient sexually because of their need for lengthy foreplay. Even the word implies this stage isn't part of the play, but work that has to be done first—before play.

It is significant that subconsciously many women have internalized this point of view. Some of the women were as surprised by experiencing a skillful lover who honored her natural pace as they were by the result—extended ecstasy for both participants.

Men's sexual nature is so powerful it defines much of his behavior. It does for women too, whether suppressed or expressed. Freud built his whole career around women's suppressed sexuality, claiming it was the father's penis that kept her stunned. Perhaps he missed the real point—her suppressed sexuality does make her neurotic, but it is the *tyranny* of his penis causing the problems, not the *existence* of his penis. In other words, a healthy whole woman is not afraid of sex, only of his domination of *her sexuality*.

### Revolution, Smevolution?

Alas, the world is a real place. Patriarchy and misogyny persist in every major contemporary society. From hidden faces to clitorectomies to bride burning to 'pro-life' murders, from forced prostitution to sex-slavery, from gansta-rap to snuff films on the internet, the world is awash in titilation and gender brutality.

Scientists now know that any species that doesn't learn to cooperate with other species on earth will perish. The biological record is clear on this. That one gender of a species would cripple the partner gender is unseen in any other species.

Some kind of metamorphosis is also going on in the broader world. The earth itself is wobbling electromagnetically, a lot. The pace of change among societies, science and technology increases so rapidly, the curve looks just like a bee-hive about to split, or an anthill under attack, or a group of lemmings about to do themselves in.

We just happen to live at this turning point, a time of transformation in the earth itself as well as in our species. Scientists see this kind of rapid change and apparent chaos as the signal of an impending major leap.

We don't know whether what we do or don't do now will be significant in the evolution of human development—only our descendents will know, and that only in retrospect.

However, when we twist the lens a little, change the angle a bit, step back into a bigger mirror, we see writing on the wall. Through science and spirituality, physics and metaphysics, we are rapidly transforming our views of nature and ourselves.

Major systems perturbations are an on-going backdrop for this generation of women, who chose to change a lot of previously accepted behavior in our society. For instance, for better or for worse, women are out of the home and into the workforce in great numbers. In one generation, they achieved some measure of economic independence, although not yet economic equality.

They redefined marriage – both the right to more easily get out of it, and the right for equal protection under the law while in it. Husbands can no longer beat their wives (or children) with impunity. The courts actually go after deadbeat fathers who don't support their children after divorce. The courts convict rapists and no longer blame their victims for the rape itself.

These changes directly relate to woman's sexuality, her sense of safety and security, her freedom to be sexually responsible for herself. They reflect a major shift in the previously pervasive laws and view of women as little more than incompetent, emotional children, who were innately irresponsible sexually.

Look at Beth in Texas in the 60s and 70s, where a woman under twenty-one was still under the protective custody of a father or husband, whatever his age. She could be committed and her marriage annulled without her consent.

Previous generations of women would call what's been accomplished in forty years a miracle. Some men see it as a major challenge to the habits of patriarchy and misogyny and fight to keep woman's power trivialized.

However, woman's sexual capacity is not vestigial, like the appendix, but is emergent, like brain size, *way beyond* the need for procreative bonding and motherhood. It is unique in nature and therefore significant *for a reason* . . . we just don't know what that is, yet.

Given Shlain's contention that women have led all the giant leaps forward in our species development so far, it makes sense that the evolution of woman's sexual awareness is *necessary* to trigger the next jump in the evolution of species consciousness. How could a species make a giant leap forward when half of that species is deliberately kept from their full potential? Here's why I think woman's sexual energy is the key:

*First,* quantum physics teaches that our bodies are primarily electro-magnetic energy waves, connected to everything at the subatomic level. Communication among the waves is instantaneous, multi-universe-wide.

A fully-aroused woman receives and channels a huge amount of raw energy into the world. This unique ability literally changes the energetic make-up of the universe—*the result is Daphne's dance.*

*Second,* we experience ecstatic states as sacred energy, whether we used meditation, self-flagellation or orgasming to get there, according to amazingly similar descriptions from diverse spiritually enlightened teachers like Rumi, Buddha, King Solomon and more. Ancient, pre-Confucian Taoists thought woman's body the bridge to immortality.

Many people who might never meditate, equate a good long orgasm with calmness, inner peace, a sense of joy, lasting hours and days. For those who experience this state regularly, orgasming within the body and brain can become a 'walking around' way to be, without any genital stimulation, like a walking meditation. Cooperation and compassion are natural modes of behavior in this state.

*Third,* each time a woman 'comes until she is insensible,' her brain shuts off fear centers, so there is literally less fear energy and more joy energy in the world.

All three of those points sound like a shift to higher-consciousness to me—female energy dancing in balance with nature, cooperation and compas-sion normal modes of being, less fear and more joy in the world.

I envision a yin/yang symbol, but one with the midline lopsided—too much white, say. I can try to *push* the midline back to balance, but it's hard to do because white energy doesn't like to give up power. Or, I could pump black energy in the until the midline returns to balance naturally, filling like a balloon.

Woman's authentic potential has been out of balance since Daphne with-drew her energy, protecting herself from the violent rape of the patriarchy. She alone can decide when she feels safe enough to return her unique energetic frequency to the mix.

Jeanne said that one night of that kind of physical ecstasy changed her self-esteem forever and all her sexual behavior since. Others describe it as a direct connection with the primal energy of the universe, leading to authentic self-love, compassion for all and amazing creative spurts.

*Metaphysics* says the way to enlightenment is *through the body*, not around the body. *Physics* says the body is actually particles randomly jumping in and out of energy waves. Ecstatic states are definitely high-frequency energy waves generated by the body, through pleasure and joy, engendering health and well-being.

So evolution or revolution? Probably both. It looks and feels like revolution because women are challenging the prevailing myths and institutionalized patriarchy. Probably evolution is responsible.

## Daphne goes first

Clearly the women in this study tell stories of a new myth. Even the potency of Cupid's arrows wears off eventually. The new myth says Daphne, the whole, sensual, sexual woman, has thoughts and values, strengths and boundaries *even when she is true to her sexual nature*. Maybe especially when she is true to herself.

Nine out of fourteen—two-thirds—of the randomly selected woman had experienced multiple and extended orgasmic states! That number just keeps going through my head and is always followed by the realization that each one of those women had a skillful lover as a partner.

Profound power hovers beneath the surface of woman's sexual capacity—both because of the amount of effort Nature has put into developing it, and the amount of effort the patriarchy has put into suppressing or trivializing it.

I believe there is an ancient, perhaps genetic, agreement between men and women that *men go first in danger*. His strengths are focused in the *tangible*. He has brought us physical safety, providing meat and protecting us from sabertooth tigers and what not. He succeeded at being more vicious than all other animals in nature, ensuring our survival.

However, we really don't need that kind of brutality anymore. Unfocused, it rechannels itself into violence in families, villages and world wars, as well as environmental destruction.

Now we need *her* strengths. She leads us into cooperation, joy and compassion. *Women go first in pleasure*. Her strengths are focused in the *intangible*. Now that we are physically safe, her gift and responsibility is the ability to channel intense high frequency pleasure so that profound changes in human consciousness itself can occur.

Occasionally when I watch the news about suicide bombers and death tolls, I indulge in this fantasy. I imagine that all political leaders, generals and corporate decision-makers, world-wide, start out every day fully, authentically, sexually satisfied. Imagine how much less greedy or angry one feels when authentically filled up!

I envision living and working around people for whom being sexually satisfied is normal, average, even assumed. Nature designed our bodies for it.

When women are fulfilled sexually, their partners usually are too. The opposite is rarely the case—when men insist on going first in pleasure, women rarely get their needs met.

She must go first and the wise women in this study told us how to do it—one orgasm at a time, one exploration into sexual capacity at a time, one decision to remain true to herself and not compromise on pleasure at a time.

This quiet revolution isn't about placards or body paint or catchy slogans. It moves forward each time a woman says to herself, 'I have the right and the responsibility to explore my sexual nature to its fullest.'

I reiterate, at this point we can only speculate on the *significance* of woman's uniqueness in nature—her clitoris, ability to say no to sex when in heat, post-menopausal libido, extended orgasmic states—and what it could mean in the evolution of consciousness.

Daphne's dilemma is about one woman at a time feeling safe enough to relax into her true nature, to *dance* a more authentic set of sexual values in the real world.

Stepping up to the sexual-equality plate is still quite dangerous for women. Men are still physically stronger, more urgent in their sexual needs.

If she says no to sex, she risks that he will turn his sexual frustrations into violence against her. If she says yes to sex, her orgasms can be longer and more intense (if she's lucky), so she risks his jealously and renewed domination or total rejection.

Can Daphne give up the safety of her tree-form for the thrill of a sacred cosmic dance? The women in this study said yes—*this is what a good girl does.* Marianne said, 'What if ultimately our highest calling is to enjoy ourselves?" What if we are meant to *be in joy?* Everybody wins.

As it is now, Shlain describes a humanity that 'staggers on like a person who has suffered a stroke that left half the body paralyzed.'

No matter what comes next, whether the changes occurring now are revolution or evolution, whether any given woman tries to sit on the sidelines or chooses to join in the dance, woman's authentic sexual awareness is the natural next step in our evolution.

Women go first in pleasure.
Ladies, do you hear the music?
The Universe is calling!

## Author's Note

Please meet me on the web at www.daphnesdance.com where you can participate in new or on-going research, add your story to the collective wisdom, ask questions, respond to ideas and offer your two-cents worth.

If you want to follow my ongoing train of thought, you can read my blog, *The Cosmic Clit* at www.drgeta.wordpress.com.

## Coming Next
### (... all puns intended)

Available early in 2010, ISyn Publications will release audio readings of the interviews included in this book.

Later in 2010, ISyn Publications will release the second book in this series by Dr. Olsen, *Beyond Orgasm,* a down-to-earth guide to ecstatic states.

# Bibliography

Cass, Vivienne Ph.D.: *The Elusive Orgasm: A Woman's guide to why she can't and how she can orgasm*, Da Capo Press, 2007

Chang, Stephen Thomas: *The Tao of Sexology: The Book of Infinite Wisdom* Tao Publishing, 1986

Chia, Mantak: *Taoist Secrets of Love: Cultivating male sexual energy;* Aurora Press, 1984

Chia, Mantak and Chia, Maneewan: *Healing Love through the Tao: Cultivating female sexual energy;* Destiny Books, 2000

Cleary, Thomas: *Immortal Sisters: Secret teachings of Taoist women;* North Atlantic Books, 1996

Estrich, Susan: *Sex and Power;* Riverhead Books. 2000

Georgiadis, J. R. et. al.: "Regional cerebral blood flow changes associated with clitorally induced orgasm in healthy women;" *European Journal of Neuroscience*, Vol. 24, pp. 3305–3316, 2006

Georgiadis, Janniko R. and Holstege, Gert; "Human Brain Activation during Sexual Stimulation of the Penis" *The Journal Of Comparative Neurology* 493:33–38 (2005)

Harvey, Andrew: *The Way of Passion: A Celebration of Rumi;* J.P. Tarcher/Putnam, New York, 1994

Houston, Jean: *Jump Time: Shaping your future in a world of radical change,* J.P. Tarcher/Putnam, New York, 2000

Kinsey, Alfred: *Sexual Behavior in the Human Male;* Indiana University Press 1949, 1998

Kinsey, Alfred: *Sexual Behavior in the Human Female;* Indiana University Press 1952, 1998

Masters and Johnson: *Human Sexuality* (5th Edition); Allyn & Bacon, 1950, 1997

Masters, Johnson and Kolodny: *Human Sexual Inadequacy;* Boston, 1970

Pfaff, D. Schober, J.: "The neurophysiology of sexual arousal" *Best Practice & Research Clinical Endocrinology & Metabolism*, Vol. 21, Issue 3, pgs. 445-461

Sheehy, Gail: *Sex and the Seasoned Woman*, Random House New York, 2006

Sahtouris, Elizabet: *EarthDance;* www.ratical.org/LifeWeb/

Shlain, Leonard: *Sex, Time and Power*, Penguin, 2003

Yudelove, Eric: *Taoist Yoga and Sexual Energy; Internal Alchemy and Chi Kung*, Llewellyn Publications 2000

Watson, Lyall: *Gifts of Unknown Things*, Destiny Books, 1991

Wiley, T.S. and Formby, Bent: *Lights Out: Sleep, sugar, and survival;* Atria 2001

# Index

www.ingramcontent.com/pod-product-compliance
Lightning Source LLC
Chambersburg PA
CBHW050117280326
41933CB00010B/1142